Instructional
Coaching*in Action*

ELLEN B.
EISENBERG

BRUCE P.
EISENBERG

ELLIOTT A.
MEDRICH

IVAN
CHARNER

Instructional
Coaching *in Action*

AN INTEGRATED APPROACH
THAT TRANSFORMS THINKING,
PRACTICE, AND SCHOOLS

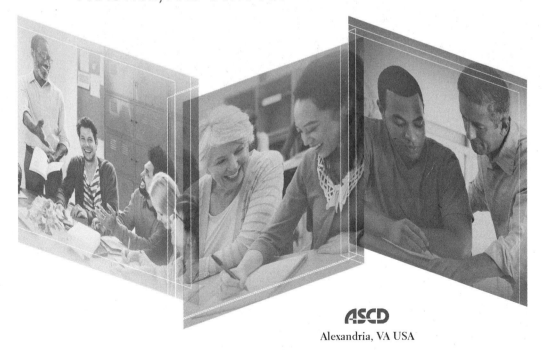

ASCD
Alexandria, VA USA

1703 N. Beauregard St. • Alexandria, VA 22311-1714 USA
Phone: 800-933-2723 or 703-578-9600 • Fax: 703-575-5400
Website: www.ascd.org • E-mail: member@ascd.org
Author guidelines: www.ascd.org/write

Deborah S. Delisle, *Executive Director*; Robert D. Clouse, *Managing Director, Digital Content & Publications*; Stefani Roth, *Publisher*; Genny Ostertag, *Director, Content Acquisitions*; Susan Hill, *Acquisitions Editor*; Julie Houtz, *Director, Book Editing & Production*; Joy Scott Ressler, *Editor*; Georgia Park, *Senior Graphic Designer*; Mike Kalyan, *Director, Production Services*; Andrea Hoffman, *Senior Production Specialist*; Valerie Younkin, *Production Designer*.

All web links in this book are correct as of the publication date below but may have become inactive or otherwise modified since that time. If you notice a deactivated or changed link, please e-mail books@ascd.org with the words "Link Update" in the subject line. In your message, please specify the web link, the book title, and the page number on which the link appears.

PAPERBACK ISBN: 978-1-4166-2368-7   ASCD product #117028   n5/17

PDF E-BOOK ISBN: 978-1-4166-2370-0; see Books in Print for other formats.

Quantity discounts are available: e-mail programteam@ascd.org or call 800-933-2723, ext. 5773, or 703-575-5773. For desk copies, go to www.ascd.org/deskcopy.

Library of Congress Cataloging-in-Publication Data
Names: Eisenberg, Ellen B., author.
Title: Instructional coaching in action : an integrated approach that transforms thinking, practice, and schools / Ellen B. Eisenberg, Bruce P. Eisenberg, Elliott A. Medrich, Ivan Charner.
Description: Alexandria, Virginia : ASCD, [2017] | Includes bibliographical references and index.
Identifiers: LCCN 2017005069 (print) | LCCN 2017018386 (ebook) | ISBN 9781416623700 (PDF) | ISBN 9781416623687 (pbk.)
Subjects: LCSH: Teachers—In-service training. | Mentoring in education. | School improvement programs.
Classification: LCC LB1731 (ebook) | LCC LB1731 .E38 2017 (print) | DDC 370.71/1—dc23
LC record available at https://lccn.loc.gov/2017005069

25 24 23 22 21 20 19 18 17   1 2 3 4 5 6 7 8 9 10 11 12

Instructional Coaching *in Action*

Acknowledgments

This book is the product of our larger endeavor to design an educator-centered approach to instructional coaching and teacher professional development.

First and foremost, we wish to thank Mrs. Lenore Annenberg of the Annenberg Foundation, who provided the grant that supported our instructional coaching journey, and Dr. Gail Levin, former executive director of the Annenberg Foundation, for believing in the power of teacher professional development as a way to build teacher capacity and improve student learning.

Many thanks also to the Annenberg Foundation and its vision in supporting capacity-building initiatives to address both the knowledge gap and the leadership gap in transforming schools. Without your continued support and philanthropy, neither the Pennsylvania High School Coaching Initiative (PAHSCI) nor the Pennsylvania Institute for Instructional Coaching (PIIC) could have existed and helped grow teacher capacity.

Thanks to our partners at the Pennsylvania Department of Education for their financial support and collaboration, especially to the Pennsylvania secretaries of education over the last 10 years for recognizing the value of and maintaining this public-private partnership that was established in 2005. We also could not have met our objectives without the support of Pennsylvania's intermediate units (regional educational service centers) and member districts that recognized the ways in which instructional coaching could serve as a vehicle to improve teacher instructional practice and student achievement.

We would also like to thank the Penn Literacy Network for helping us define the literacy component of our educator-centered instructional coaching framework and provide related, ongoing professional development through the University of

Pennsylvania Graduate School of Education, and our fiscal organizations, the Philadelphia Foundation and Capital Area Intermediate Unit, which provided oversight and financial direction throughout the duration of our work.

And last but not least, many thanks and great appreciation to Erin Saunders, our PIIC Communications Coordinator, who kept us on track and ensured that we were prepared for each review. She read with an "editor's eye" as we moved forward.

This work was a collective endeavor. We were supported by the teachers, coaches, mentors, regional mentor coordinators, Pennsylvania Intermediate Unit staff, and PIIC consultants. This large group of committed educators helped us gather the collective wisdom in the room and design an instructional coaching framework for changing thinking, practice, and schools. We are indebted to them for their dedication and determination in keeping students at the center and helping teachers change practice.

Introduction

Ensuring student success requires a new kind of teaching, conducted by teachers who understand learning and pedagogy, who can respond to the needs of their students and the demands of their disciplines, and who can develop strong connections between students' experiences and the goals of the curriculum. Efforts to improve student achievement can succeed only by building the capacity of teachers to improve their instructional practice and the capacity of school systems to promote teacher learning.

—Linda Darling-Hammond, *Professional Learning in the Learning Profession*

We all agree: students need great teachers. There is much less agreement, however, on exactly what a great teacher is or how to make certain that every teacher is great or that every student is taught by a great teacher. After all, what do we mean by "great"?

Currently, many policymakers argue that too many teachers are poorly prepared for the challenge of the classroom. For this and other reasons, they say, schools are unable to provide a quality education to all children.

In fact, we can promote teacher learning now and make certain that teachers have the opportunity to explore and learn new practices, grow on the job, and deliver better instruction to their students. In particular, we believe that our model, educator-centered instructional coaching (ECIC), can help change the teaching dynamic in schools and classrooms. We may need to do many things to ensure that every student has a great teacher, but at least we can start by changing the way we think about professional development and professional learning. *To improve student outcomes, we need to transform the way we think about teaching, learning, and how to help teachers grow as professionals.* To improve instructional practice, we must recognize that not every teacher is an expert on teaching methods, pedagogy, and subject matter content, but most are eager and committed to doing their jobs well. The challenge is to make changes in schools that offer teachers the support that will help them meet their teaching and student learning goals.

Fundamentally, educator-centered instructional coaching is based on an abiding respect for teachers and school leaders as professionals who are always interested in improving their practice. Our framework appreciates everyone as a learner and a member of a community of practice. It is not designed to bail out troubled teachers or troubled schools. It is not intended to meet one-time needs of teachers or school leaders. It is a commitment that supports the sustainable changes in practice that help teachers and school leaders redefine their goals for schoolwide improvement and puts effective practices in place that transform teaching and learning over the long term.

Why Our Educator-Centered Instructional Coaching Model Is Unique

All models of coaching share some common elements, and some aspects of our framework are certainly familiar to those who have explored the theory and practice of coaching. That said, the following points summarize the distinguishing features of our model:

- Our framework recognizes that coaching is an increasingly accepted practice in schools, and we promote the valued role of coaching as a way of delivering job-embedded professional development. Our framework focuses on helping teachers and school leaders improve instructional practice in ways that have an impact on student engagement and student learning.
- The key to our framework, the BDA (before-during-after) cycle of consultation, makes professional learning collaborative and helps coaches address the needs of teachers and school leaders in a way that is confidential and non-evaluative. *Those who are coached set the agenda.* The framework promotes a change of culture. It recognizes and respects the professional—the teacher or school leader—as the source of engagement. It is not about "fixing" anyone; it is about building people's capacity on their own terms through a collaborative process, in one-on-one or small-group settings.
- Embedded in adult-learning theory, ECIC emphasizes four key interdependent areas of practice: (1) applying evidence-based literacy practices; (2) focusing on data collection and analysis; (3) promoting nonevaluative, confidential collaboration and reflection; and (4) supporting coaches through mentoring. These practices are the centerpiece of one-on-one and small-group

support throughout the BDA cycle. Although these practices are not unique, their continual presence distinguishes our coaching model from others. Every time a coach meets with a teacher, *evidence-based literacy practices* designed to improve instruction are a focal point, as are *collecting, analyzing, and applying data*, and a *structured, nonevaluative effort at reflection*.

Instructional coaching can help teachers change the teaching and learning equation. At this time—when practitioners are more aware than ever of how much needs to be done within classrooms and schools to improve the quality of teaching—altering professional support of teaching is crucial for schoolwide improvement. Some seek the transformation of teacher education and induction programs. Eventually those efforts will make an impact. Realistically, however, if we want to see improvements for this generation of students, we will need to boost the skills of a large percentage of the 3.5 million teachers working in our schools today (U.S. Department of Education, 2016). Teachers need a professional learning lifeline *now*.

Our Journey

This book is the product of practice and experience over many years. In 2005, the Annenberg Foundation and the Pennsylvania Department of Education partnered to develop a statewide system of instructional coaching. The objective of the collaboration was to prepare and support coaches who provide job-embedded professional development for teachers on building their instructional practice and pedagogical skills.

In 2010, the Annenberg Foundation and the Pennsylvania Department of Education extended the project, and the Pennsylvania Institute for Instructional Coaching (PIIC) began supporting coaches through regional education agencies called *intermediate units* (IUs) across Pennsylvania. At this time, 25 of the state's 29 regional agencies participate, and many hundreds of instructional coaches are implementing the PIIC model of educator-centered instructional coaching and consistent professional development in their school communities.

This continuing relationship and investment has convinced school leaders around the state that PIIC's approach substantially helps teachers improve their instructional practices and strengthens school cultures that embrace continuous improvement. Our work is no longer limited to Pennsylvania. Today, coaches, administrators, and others interested in the transformation of teaching and learning in all 50 states and 30-plus countries use resources we provide through our websites and blogs (PIIC, 2016).

The educator-centered instructional coaching model, designed by PIIC, evolved over a six-year period. PIIC also provides ongoing professional development to instructional coaches on four core elements: one-on-one and small-group support; evidence-based literacy practices applied across all content areas; data collection, analysis, and application; and nonevaluative reflection on practice—all provided by coaches to teachers and other school leaders. PIIC-trained instructional coaches offer teachers tools and support to help them improve their practice and deliver quality instruction. As part of their training, PIIC coaches are also supported by mentors who receive ongoing professional development to bolster their own skills.

How This Book Is Organized

This book explores our concept of instructional coaching and suggests action steps for implementation. Chapters describe the roots and the basics of coaching and of our framework. We examine instructional coaching in action, beginning with the complex task of laying the groundwork for this approach to professional development. Subsequent chapters explore the elements of selecting, training, and supporting coaches. Throughout the book, we place instructional coaching into the larger conversation around school change and school transformation.

We welcome you on this journey to discover important new processes, tools, and practices that make a difference in student-learning outcomes—one classroom at a time.

1

Coaching — Not Just for Athletes

No one expects an athlete or a musician to become great without a coach—an over-the-shoulder mentor who pushes and supports, watches and intervenes at critical moments, analyzes learners' actions and challenges them to become self-critical analysts of their own performances. Just so with teaching. It is a demanding craft, requiring of its practitioners both careful planning and finely tuned adaptation to the flow of classroom activity and conversation. The craft can be learned, but not from a textbook. It must be learned through guided practice.

—Lauren Resnick, Foreword in *Content-Focused Coaching*

Everyone knows, or at least knows of, a coach. Most of us think we know, or know of, a good coach. Although we may not all agree on what makes a coach "good," most of us think that we know one when we see one.

Whether it is a big-time coach of a favorite professional or college sports team, the coach of a Little League team, an executive coach helping a CEO find ways to improve her leadership skills, a voice coach helping an aspiring vocalist, a life coach, or one of the many other kinds of coaches that are now ubiquitous in our culture, there is no longer anything exceptional about the concept of coaching. One study estimated that 90 percent of organizations with more than 2,000 employees made regular use of coaches (Institute of Leadership and Management, 2011).

Coaching is well recognized as a way to support a wide variety of professionals. Regardless of the kind of coaching, those doing it are all trying to accomplish the same result—to help those with whom they work grow in a job-embedded setting. The coaches all want to help their teaching colleagues go from good to great—that is, to help them refine their practices.

This is no different for the teachers and administrators who make up our own professional community, which begs two simple questions: Because so many

1

professions recognize coaching for its valued contribution to the growth and development of skill and talent, why is it not generally accepted as a powerful tool among educators? And why aren't all teachers and school leaders coached to help nurture their own professional growth? After all, the data, though limited, strongly indicate that coaching can strengthen practice and give teachers confidence to try new things in their classrooms.

Coaching in Schools

There are no estimates of the number of coaches in schools today. Certainly, many work in subject-specific content areas, focusing on helping teachers successfully implement particular program initiatives. In these instances, coaches are essential because they can help schools get the most out of programs they adopt. The coach is recognized and accepted as an important and valuable resource.

We should ask why educators support coaching in these cases but are less willing to use coaches to help all teachers generally improve their instructional practice. If they did so, teachers would be on a par with other professionals—that is, coaching would become a tool to promote ongoing job-embedded professional growth. It would address the "whole" of teaching and learning in ways that highlight current trends in education and help teachers become better at their craft.

Whatever the particular elements and strategies associated with any single coaching model in schools, the intellectual underpinning all coaches bring to their work is well understood—coaches are committed to raising the quality of teaching and ultimately the learning outcomes for the students of coached teachers. Coaching is an investment in the improvement of practice and learning. Good coaching is not based on a deficit or "fix-it" model. Coaches are experienced teaching professionals who understand instruction, recognize effective instructional practices, assess data, and engage in ongoing conversations that ebb and flow depending on where the participants are in their professional practice. Coaches also understand that they are not experts; they are willing participants in a collaborative process that requires considerable time, consistent relationships, great leadership, and lots of humor.

Coaching in schools draws heavily on the general principles of coaching but refines these principles to align with school environments. Joellen Killion and her colleagues (Killion, Harrison, Bryan, & Clifton, 2012) offer important insights into the ingredients essential to coaching in schools: strong leadership, a clear focus and goals, essential resources, a well-prepared staff, ongoing measures to monitor progress, and rigorous evaluations. In addition to these fundamental elements, our instructional coaching framework shares some underlying beliefs with other models that promote coaching in schools:

- Coaching is professional development, and coaching is often more likely to help teachers improve practice and student learning than other forms of in-service training.
- Teachers' beliefs and philosophies need to be understood and respected by coaches, and these beliefs have a significant impact on teaching practice.
- Teachers need time to reflect on what they learn in the coaching process, what they learn from their experience in classrooms, and how they will apply these new learnings.
- Data—at the individual student, classroom, and school level—are important to the process of coaching.
- Although students are at the center of the coaching equation, there are a variety of ways to help students grow, and the most effective ways involve helping teachers improve their skills.
- Behind every effective coach is a cooperative and supportive school leader who recognizes the power of coaching.

Instructional coaching is intended to reinforce teachers' and administrators' practices in ways that support schools so that instruction is rigorous, delivery is effective, and assessment is appropriate for student learning to improve. In some cases, it helps expand both the teachers' and administrators' knowledge base; sometimes coaches help teachers and administrators use what they know to implement more-effective instructional strategies and techniques. Whatever the reason, efficacious instructional coaching builds teacher capacity, influences what students learn, increases student engagement, and helps both teachers and their students become more successful learners.

The Educator-Centered Instructional Coaching Framework

A coach's role is to help teachers, in nonevaluative and confidential ways, to implement effective instructional practices. Coaches help teachers identify their strengths and, working together, strategize ways to bolster practice. They help teachers recognize their voices and take ownership of their learning. They must coach on any given topic, not just in the coach's area of expertise. They work directly with teachers at the level that makes a difference—the classroom. Sometimes they are mistakenly identified as "fixers." But that is not the instructional coach's objective. Coaches do not provide a silver bullet that can address all that plagues our educational system.

If that were true, we would bottle it and sell it! Some even think that just because teachers went to college they shouldn't need coaches. Yet they accept that professional athletes and musicians, who are at the top of their professions, are encouraged and sometimes required to be coached.

Our framework, educator-centered instructional coaching, or ECIC, rests heavily on the premise that professional growth is a career-long process. It is never "done." A teacher can always become better by working with a coach. Remember, every year teachers work with different groups of students with diverse learning needs. Working with instructional coaches provides ongoing opportunities for teachers to collaborate, practice, and learn together. They apply all they have learned to each new situation and create new learning experiences, all with the support and assistance of a coach, a skilled and knowledgeable practitioner.

Professional development for teachers has meaning only insofar as it informs teaching and learning. In our view, coaches provide the essential lynchpin that personalizes professional development to meet each teacher's needs as a classroom instructor. Thus, ECIC is much more than the antithesis of the "one-shot" or the "fix-it" mode of professional development. It embodies all of Killion's principles and builds on them with certain break-the-mold principles and practices. Specifically, it is:

- Designed to move teachers and schools from professional development (the "stuff" teachers learn) to professional learning (how deeply they learn "it" and how well these learnings are applied in other contexts).
- Structured as an interconnected combination of process, pedagogy, practice, and content that together support continuous teacher professional development and learning.
- Designed to meet the individual needs of teachers and to reflect their "voice" through one-on-one and small-group support received from their coach.
- Committed to the strictly nonevaluative and protective nature of teacher privacy so that coaches are accepted as helpers, not evaluators.
- Based on quality standards at several levels of leadership—for teachers, for coaches, and for mentors to coaches.
- Focused on applying the school's evidence-based literacy practices across all content areas.

Because most evidence suggests that short-term gains in student outcomes do not lead to long-term success (Grissmer, Beekman, & Ober, 2014), our coaching model is designed to provide ongoing, continual support to produce long-term gains by helping teachers and school leaders rethink and change their practice.

Coaching is a relationship between two equals—teacher and coach—both of whom are committed to making personal and professional improvement. A coaching relationship provides the opportunity for reciprocity of gifts of knowledge and skill, caring, and support (Barkley, 2010).

This is a different message about professional development. It offers a chance to throw out the traditional playbook and rethink how to best help teachers do their best work and improve their capacity to meet the needs of their students, regardless of the content. We believe that instructional coaching, effectively implemented, helps build instructional practices across all content areas, especially with the targeted focus of literacy.

A Basic Tenet of ECIC: Understanding Adult Learners

With ECIC, instructional coaches and teachers work together in real time to plan, deliver, and debrief about practice. (In our lexicon, the debriefing process is a non-evaluative analysis of action.) Educator-centered instructional coaching provides consistency in language and practice to minimize variations between teachers in the same school and to facilitate sharing the vision for schoolwide improvement. Teachers and coaches collaborate regularly, discussing effective instructional strategies, tackling everyday problems of practice, and learning from each other. Colleagues provide specific feedback and thought-provoking discussions designed to improve practice, build teacher capacity, increase student engagement, and improve student learning.

Educator-centered instructional coaching is about adults collaborating with adults. To be effective, coaches have to understand how adults learn. The skill sets required to engage and support adults are complicated. Coaches need to be knowledgeable in at least one subject area—their own; they must be skilled in the art of questioning because establishing relationships with other adults is based on asking questions to gain understanding; and they must demonstrate that they, too, are members in a community of practice and learning. They must be active learners, recognize the differences in how adults and adolescents learn, be receptive to varying opinions and perspectives, and make teachers aware that they can establish their own learning patterns—which includes making mistakes. That's how learning occurs, but through very different processes for adults.

One might think that teachers—who foster others' learning for a living—would welcome new learning themselves. Yet many adults do not realize that their own learning can improve, which, of course, would result in improved learning for their students. We want teachers to recognize that their learning is multifaceted; that is, their learning is not just about their own subject matter but involves expanding their knowledge base and the variety of learning opportunities available to them. This kind of "teacher learning" occurs through working with coaches, adult to adult. As Malcolm Knowles suggests, "... instruction for adults needs to focus more on the process and less on the content being taught. Strategies such as case studies, role-playing, simulations, and self-evaluation are most useful" (as cited in Mulholland & Turnock, 2013, p. 16). Instructional coaches apply all of these strategies in their work with teachers, helping them to broaden their own experiences through practice and to understand how this learning is related to student growth. Here is how a coach described her experience.

Side-by-Side Learning

I didn't realize that as I was working to support and enhance a teacher's skill set and knowledge base, I was also nourishing my own professional development and learning. I was asking the teacher to dig deeper and think of alternate ways to accomplish his classroom goals. At the same time, I had to dig deeper into my repertoire of quality questioning skills to ask the right kind of questions that elicited a change in his thinking. My thinking changed at the same time, and I learned alongside the teacher!

Coaches need to help teachers understand that their way of learning differs from how adolescents learn. Familiarity with the principles of adult learning is a start; capacity to actualize these principles is something more. Whereas student learning is mostly passive and classroom based, adults tend to learn best when they are self-directed and engaged in solving problems they are experiencing. Adults want their learning to be relevant to the work they are doing—goal-oriented and designed to meet their needs. Process and content are practical. The basics of adult learning and how it differs from adolescent learning are summarized in the table in Figure 1.1, and although the principles are not hard to grasp, the practice often is.

Coaches who are quite comfortable coaching in their own area of certification may not be as comfortable in content areas that are unrelated to their field of expertise. However, their familiarity and knowledge base about adult learning reminds them to honor the teacher's expertise, understand the teacher's motivation for learning, ensure that the learning is relevant, and co-create learning goals that are manageable. Coaches need to know that the teachers understand their own personal learning styles and needs as well as their students' learning styles and needs. They must share the idea that if every student can learn, every adult can learn as well.

Figure 1.1 How Adult and Child Learners Differ

Adults	Children
• Classroom learning is just one of many learning modes.	• Classroom-based learning is the dominant mode.
• Motivation for learning: career, qualifications, direct knowledge needed to do a job.	• Learning for advancement.
• Adults seek learning that has meaning for them at a given point in time.	• Children have compulsory attendance for the majority of their learning experience.
• Emphasis on self-directed learning.	• Teacher driven.
• Learning is collaborative and facilitated and often problem based.	• Learning is often passive and dependent.
• Adults bring lifelong experience to the subject matter.	• Children do not bring broad life experiences to learning.
• Adults often have strong values and need to unlearn or have their values challenged.	• Children's values are less well developed.

Source: From "The Adult Learner May Really Be a Neglected Species," by Sean O'Toole and Belinda Essex, April 2012, *Australian Journal of Adult Learning, 52*(1), p. 190. Copyright 2012 by the Australian Journal of Adult Learning. Adapted with permission.

Four Key Areas of Practice

The four key areas of practice of ECIC—evidence-based literacy practices; data collection and analysis; nonevaluative, confidential collaboration, and self-reflection; and supporting coaches through mentoring—are interconnected. All are delivered from coach to teacher and from mentor to coach via one-on-one and small-group interactions using the BDA (before-during-after) cycle of consultation that we mentioned in the Introduction to this book and that is described further later in this chapter.

Key Practice Area 1: Evidence-Based Literacy Practices

Educator-centered instructional coaches strive to continuously stay on top of effective evidenced-based literacy practices, and their conversations with teachers often focus on practices that reinforce the importance of reading, writing, speaking, and listening across all content areas. The literacy focus is not about teaching reading; it is about the process of helping adult learners understand the importance of reading to learn and building on each student's prior knowledge and literacy skills, not just the content of their subjects. Most schools have adopted an evidenced-based literacy program, an essential component in implementing an effective instructional coaching model. Working with their school's program, instructional coaches collaborate with their teaching colleagues to ensure that students are able to interact with their text, derive meaning from what they read, and apply what they've learned in multiple contexts. The coach reinforces teachers' understanding of the school literacy program and helps them apply the literacy principles and practices to their own content.

Remember that coaches are skilled at coaching those literacy principles and practices, *not* necessarily subject matter content. Their goal is to help all teachers improve practice without regard to subject matter. That said, one of the things that makes ECIC unique is that the work, by its nature, promotes literacy—reading, writing, speaking, listening, and thinking—across the curriculum, in every classroom and with every teacher, regardless of their subject matter expertise. The process of developing this broad definition of literacy is recursive and requires teachers to be deliberate and purposeful in supporting their students. Instructional coaches help teachers understand that process and help them identify appropriate strategies to reinforce effective instruction in their content areas. Consider the following example involving an instructional coach, literacy skills, and science content.

Literacy and Science

When Ms. Mallen began coaching, she met first with the teachers in the science department. For several weeks, she worked to help them understand the importance of literacy in helping students understand science concepts rather than coaching on content-specific matters. Many of the teachers responded with, "I'm not a reading teacher, and we have content to cover before testing." She replied, "Our goal is to reinforce the notion that students must read to learn and build on the literacy practices that help them succeed. By implementing some new evidence-based literacy strategies, we can help students understand more about interacting and engaging with their text as well as about specific science content. If we teach strategies that develop students' awareness and knowledge of science concepts, we can expand our students' ability to apply their learning in a variety of scientific environments."

Some colleagues were reluctant to work one-on-one with Ms. Mallen, so she met with small groups and described several literacy strategies to help students navigate the science content. For example, she shared ideas of how to help students with academic vocabulary, the words that were critical to understanding science concepts. She showed the teachers how to use a variety of instructional strategies, as well as ideas about partnering and grouping students so they could benefit from "social learning." She showed her colleagues how to help students focus on text features in their textbooks and how the organization of the chapters could help them predict the content in the assigned sections. She continually reminded the teachers that she was not the expert, that they all had expertise to share and that she was capitalizing on their content knowledge and marrying that with different instructional strategies. She modeled how she reflected on her actions and when she noticed that adjustments in her practice were needed. She was eventually successful in helping her colleagues think about how to help students read, write, and think like scientists.

Educator-centered instructional coaching recognizes that working one-on-one and in small groups focusing on evidence-based literacy practices, reflective practices, and data collection practices across all content areas helps to build teacher capacity and support student learning. Sometimes the outcome has a broader impact. Consider, for instance, a teacher who identifies classroom management as an issue. The coach and teacher meet to discuss the concern, understanding that classroom management is often a function of effective lesson design (which, ideally, incorporates evidence-based literacy practices). That is, when students are actively involved and engaged in the learning process, classroom management problems diminish. The following example illustrates how one coach helped a teacher to deal with this issue.

Lesson Design, Literacy, and Classroom Management

When the French teacher asked me to schedule some time with her, I was thrilled. She knew my content area was math and thought that like math, French had academic vocabulary, symbols, and a language all its own.

At our first meeting, we talked about her perception of the students she taught. I asked her how she would assess their skill set, interest level, and knowledge base. I knew she was motivated to make changes, and she readily admitted that she was having difficulty managing her class. She typically assigned several tasks that needed to be graded and predicated each day's work on the papers she evaluated the previous night. Many days, she could not get to the papers even though the next day's classwork revolved around the homework, making her feel scattered and unprepared because she couldn't change direction midstream. The students became disinterested and disruptive because the work was either too difficult or not challenging enough. Either way, she knew she needed some support in managing her work and her students.

The first thing we did was to take a look at what she thought were essential topics to teach and if she thought her students were able to handle the curriculum requirements. Then we discussed the goals that were associated with each topic—for example, what she wanted students to know and be able to do related to the topics, what she needed to know about those topics, and what her students needed to know about those topics. We compared the lists and discussed where they intersected, how we would help the students get "ready" to learn, and what resources would help her prepare for moving student learning forward.

Through our conversations, she recognized that her students were disruptive because the way she approached their learning was not aligned to how they needed to learn. She needed to spend more time thinking about what they needed to learn, how she was going to help them learn, the resources and materials she would use, how she would assess their learning, and what she would do with the students who did not move forward. She needed to realize when the students were "lost" and to stop, look, and listen to their needs.

Additionally, we talked about a variety of student engagement techniques that could be useful. She especially liked the think/pair/share strategies and the idea of asking her students to demonstrate their understanding through alternative assessments that incorporated various forms of literacy, such as creating menus and travel brochures in French when they talked about geographic locations, assuming the persona of a meteorologist delivering the weather in French, writing a police report detailing a robbery at the Louvre, or creating a playbill for a play at a local theater. She generated several ideas when she started thinking about various ways to help students see the relevance of the content and translate their ideas from English into

French. These were resources she and her students could create and that would make the learning more meaningful than just reading a textbook.

Within three months, the teacher and her students felt as if they were in a new environment. We were eventually able to bring in other language teachers so they could collaborate on effective instructional practices and experience the same success as the French teacher.

Key Practice Area 2: Data Collection and Analysis

In the past, school professionals had little access to information that could help them understand the needs of their students. That no longer is the case. Educators are inundated with data. Their problem is not too little data, but too much. Therefore, it is crucial to analyze data *with purpose*. Skilled coaches help teachers figure out what is germane to their needs and what is not, what is of strategic interest and what is "noise." Of course, this approach assumes that coaches themselves know how to analyze data. Furthermore, as former teachers (which most coaches are), instructional coaches often are not initially accustomed to looking at *someone else's* data—data related to students of teachers they are coaching—and figuring out how the information might apply to a given teaching and learning problem. This is a good example of why coaches themselves need professional development opportunities. In their own professional learning, instructional coaches become more knowledgeable and skillful in looking at data and recognizing what is important in a particular situation. They learn strategies, such as working with groups of teachers in the same grade or subject to share data and find patterns, and they learn how to help teachers learn what to look for in their own classroom situations. Here is an example of how one coach has dealt with the data analysis aspect of the coaching role.

Dealing with Data

Data are a great access point. Coaches need to explore schoolwide data first so that their colleagues understand that the goals for the work are aligned with schoolwide objectives. When I first started coaching, the principal gave me a packet of data by grade, content area, and teacher and requested that I meet with each teacher and talk about the quarter grades and the number of students failing in each teacher's classroom. Of course, this was a monumental task and not particularly useful to anyone. Talking about data is not just about the numbers; talking about data is really talking about how teachers teach and students learn. Talking about the number of students failing instead of talking about why some students are successful and others are not doesn't get to the heart of implementing effective instructional practices.

So, given the task at hand, I started with the data from a small group of 9th grade teachers and their students. I prepared myself by looking at the source of the data, standardized test scores, and creating a chart with a gap analysis to see where the students were having the most trouble—that is, which content areas or topics within the content areas seemed most problematic. Then I reviewed the chart and decided to focus on one content area only but brought together all the teachers in that grade-level team so that we could introduce an interdisciplinary approach to student learning. My thinking was that if we could start a discussion thread about the gaps in student performance, we could build on the cumulative effect that would happen if all the teachers understood that what occurred in one class affected what happened in another class.

This process took some time, and I repeated it for several months with each of the 9th grade teachers. It became easier as we moved forward because the teachers were familiar with the goals and more confident that they could do something concrete to change student outcomes. This was small-group coaching that generated several one-on-one interactions once my teaching colleagues became acclimated to using data to impact instructional decisions.

It is important to remember that "data" encompass a wide variety of kinds of information, including classroom data, schoolwide data, and specific teacher and student data. Data can be collected to create a snapshot in time, or it can be collected to paint a more nuanced picture or track progress over time. Confusion on this point is common, and we have found it essential to help coaches recognize the many kinds of information that can be useful.

Notes from a teacher meeting or a classroom visit, for instance, are valuable data in the same way that formative and summative test results on a lesson are data. These data are reflective and help coaches and teachers collaborate about moving practice forward. Coaches need data so they can design a plan of action. Teachers need data to help them make instructional decisions. For example, schoolwide data about graduation rates and promotion rates are individual and collective. Both individual teachers and schoolwide programs need to address those areas. Demographic data are also important. If a school has an influx of second-language learners, it needs to adopt a plan for intervention and support for the students. Without that data, those needs would not be recognized or addressed.

Data related to student and teacher perceptions are essential. The entire school community should know how teachers and students feel about the school climate, culture, and programs of study. Collected data reflect the voices of the constituents and need to be heard. Are there enough programs to support student needs? Is there an effective professional development plan for teachers that is supported by the instructional coach? Are teachers' voices and choices honored with attention to what matters most—student learning? Are professional learning communities established by interest rather than directive? Are goals for schoolwide improvement realistic and attainable? Are student and teacher focus groups instituted with regularity and sustainability so that the data collected are used to move practice forward?

The conversation between coach and teacher needs to include questions about what the teacher wants to accomplish in the classroom. This happens in the *before* conversation of the before-during-after cycle, when the coach and teacher identify areas of need and interest for data collection; for example, how many times does the teacher call on only the students with their hands raised in the front of the class, or which students are actively engaged in the group process and which are not. These are examples of data points that the coach and teacher agree the coach should collect when visiting the class in the *during* phase of their work. And those data become a significant part of the debriefing in the *after* conversation.

Coaches help teachers use five key objectives in collecting and using data:
1. Sharing learning intentions
2. Asking questions that show evidence of learning
3. Providing feedback that changes instruction
4. Helping teachers and students use self-assessment strategies
5. Helping teachers adjust their instruction so that students learn more and can show what they have learned

We know that data are the foundation for continuous improvement when used appropriately so that teachers can rethink what they do and how they do it, and by so doing better serve their students' needs. Coaches collaborate with teachers about what data to collect and how to use it. Coaches and teachers use data to talk about how students learn and which effective practices address the myriad of learning styles in any classroom. In these ways, coaches help teachers see the connections among data collection, research, teacher practices, and student achievement.

Key Practice Area 3: Nonevaluative, Confidential Collaboration, and Self-Reflection

The demands on teachers and school leaders are extraordinary, and a typical day can overwhelm even the most experienced educators. There is often little or no time to reflect. Instructional coaches try to bridge that gap. Coaching works best when those who are coached have a guarantee of confidentiality, which encourages them to experiment with new ideas in a risk-free environment (see Chapter 6 for more about confidentiality), as well as an opportunity to step back and reflect on what they are learning from their relationship with a coach and what they realize from applying what they have learned in their classrooms (Loughran, 2002). In the ECIC model, coaches visit classrooms and speak with teachers using nonevaluative language and encouraging self-reflection. This is quite different from administrative observations in which teachers are evaluated according to their district's parameters.

The ECIC framework promotes reflection as an essential mode of inquiry. The process itself is learned; it does not happen automatically by saying "OK, now it's time to reflect." Being *encouraged* to reflect is not enough; and stepping back and thinking about "how things are going" is not enough. Good reflective practice is structured and nonevaluative; it is a way of examining how our assumptions influence our approach to practice and our practice itself. It is a learned process of questioning and analysis that leads to new ways of understanding (Loughran, 2002). And the process matters as much as the reflection itself. Reflection repositions the teacher as a learner, and the key is for teachers and coaches alike to *make* time—not *find* time—to reflect on what they are saying and hearing while visiting or modeling. The coach's goal is to help teachers think about their instructional decisions and reflect "on, in, and about" what works in classrooms. (See Chapter 4 for more about reflection.)

Reflection is an integral part of the coach's role. It is the process during which the coach answers these questions: *What am I doing to help teachers increase student engagement? How am I helping them to improve student outcomes? How am I helping them to reach their fullest learning potential?* Answering these questions helps coaches focus on the needs of individuals, the collective school community, and their own needs as they help transform teaching and learning. Effective reflective practice leads to action on that understanding. As Kierkegaard noted, "The irony of life is that it is lived forward but understood backward."

Key Practice Area 4: Supporting Coaches through Mentoring

Coaches must be adept at collaborating and discussing issues of practice with teachers and school leaders; they will be asked to provide many different kinds of support. To accomplish this, they need to be highly skilled practitioners themselves.

To ensure their own professional growth, coaches must have a steady source of professional development opportunities to draw from as they work with teachers. The coaches' professional development becomes the teachers' professional development as they provide turn-around training to teachers and other school staff. Just as one-on-one and small-group coaching is the central feature of our framework, ongoing support and preparation of coaches is essential to their effectiveness.

Unfortunately, many coaching models assume that coaches know everything and can coach anything. As a result, school leaders are often misled, especially when coaches are introduced as experts and expected to meet a wide variety of staff needs. Coaches are highly accomplished *at coaching*; they are skilled and experienced practitioners who understand adult learning theory and are committed to helping teachers develop their own competence. But, as previously noted, they are not content experts. It follows that if the coach provides opportunities for the teacher to learn more, the same opportunity needs to be extended to the coach. Everyone on staff is a member in a community of learning and practice.

The ECIC model includes strong support for coaches from highly trained professionals who serve as mentors, helping coaches build their capacity to meet the needs of their school, the teachers, and the school leaders. Although this may appear to add a bureaucratic level to the coaching process, that is not the case. Providing coaches with support—coaches of their own—is invaluable to their growth. We have not seen circumstances where coaches, left entirely on their own, can successfully respond to the changing needs of an entire school staff. (See Chapter 10 for more on mentors for coaches.)

Coaches—More Than Resource Providers

Our discussion of the four key areas of practice leads to an important point about a function that is part of the coach's role but by no means its entirety. Through the Internet and the plethora of professional publications, coaches routinely find articles and research studies that address various classroom topics. The role of resource provider may offer access to classrooms in the beginning of the coaching relationship, but the relationship does not end there. Resources do not change practice. Coaches need to stay proactive, meeting with teachers regularly to discuss what they want their students to know and be able to do as per the goals and objectives of a lesson or unit. By providing ample opportunities to meet, plan, deliver, and debrief, coaches collaborate with teachers to identify which evidence-based strategies are most likely to work. The objective is for coaches to share research and demonstrate effective strategies that encourage teachers to try new ways of approaching instructional content without fear of failing.

Teachers benefit from the coach's exploration of articles offering evidence-based strategies that can be tailored and adapted to meet the needs of individual classrooms. Bringing teachers together to explore when and how to use those resources encourages teachers to collectively problem-solve and engage in professional conversations about what inspires student growth. The *conversations* around the resources are what results in classroom changes, not the resources themselves.

If the coaching roles and responsibilities are not clearly explained and shared with the staff, they might think that the coach's role is limited to providing resources without talking about why or how these resources are used. Remember, the coach is not just a resource provider. Consider the following example.

Going Beyond Resources

In an early coaching situation where the coaching model was being introduced, the principal explained to the staff that I was the coach and would help them identify resources to use in classrooms, and that he fully expected to see evidence that these new resources were being used when he conducted his observations. He ended by saying, "Now, please see her [the coach] and get as many resources as you can to help you teach your content. And if you write a response to one article that was given to you, then you don't have to attend the next two professional development sessions that she offers."

Wow! That relegated me to being no more than a "seek and find" provider with no hope of engaging my teaching colleagues in thoughtful conversations about teaching and learning. I knew I had about 30 seconds to dispel that erroneous view and repair it.

Not wanting to say anything that would be construed as insubordination, I stood up and explained that, indeed, I would have various resources to share but that I hoped we could learn together and discover not only resources but also ways to address our schoolwide goals for improvement.

I wanted to make a point that teachers were their own best resources and that I supported their learning and wanted to help them create effective learning environments. I continued by saying that instructional coaching was a three-pronged process (think BDA cycle) and that in the subsequent days, I would share my coaching role and responsibilities in small groups. I did not condone nor condemn the principal's directive and hoped that my comment was nonthreatening, enticing, and appealing to them.

Over the next few weeks, I made my rounds first with my "friends," whom I hoped would become my emissaries of goodwill and would spread the word that I was more than a resource provider. These were the same colleagues with whom I shared some interesting resources, and while I handed the articles and links to them, I asked if we could "touch base in a few days and share our collective thoughts on the resources and how we could use them." I also told each of them when I was going to use the highlighted resource and invited them to come to my class to see the resource "in action." (I did some homework and knew when each person had a planning period so that my offer would coincide with that time.)

I also mentioned that I would love to see how they used the resources and welcomed an opportunity to come to their classrooms. This was trickier because I didn't want to substantiate the practice of me walking into classrooms without the benefit of a *before* session where our goals, roles, and expectations were identified. I have to say, this did work, though, as some of my colleagues were eager to show me that they didn't "need" to work with a coach, while others wanted to see what I was doing in class. In this case, curiosity made the difference!

With the first few colleagues who invited me into their classrooms, I indicated that I would love an opportunity to talk to them about what they did and how they did "it." As I left their classrooms, I mentioned that I was available to talk the next day. This happened a handful of times—enough to get my feet wet and help me move toward one-on-one consultations following a more structured approach to instructional design. Those conversations morphed into discussions about why a particular resource was better than another and how a variation on delivery might make a difference in student outcomes. They asked about the resources, but the conversation that ensued was the driver of the interaction.

Although I worked hard to get my first adopters, going through the process of inviting my colleagues to my classroom demonstrated my willingness to "go first" and accept change. They did not see me as a threat because I opened my doors to them. They realized that I was asking them to not only accept my role as a coach but to let me see their work as well. Providing resources as an access point served the purpose well as long as I was able to follow that with the conversations about practice, which was my intended purpose.

The Before-During-After Cycle: The Strategic Heart of ECIC

Of the many characteristics essential to effective coaching, being a good listener and understanding the dynamics of collaboration top the list. Coaches listen and respond in ways that help teachers learn rather than just blindly accept what they are told. As Stephen Barkley notes, "Listening builds the relationship; listening allows for nuance and nonverbal communication to be 'heard'; listening allows for clarity; and listening ensures trust" (Barkley, 2010, p. 74).

In our practice, we implement the four components of our approach throughout what we call the before-during-after cycle of consultation with teachers. The cycle builds the kind of relationship Barkley describes, and it provides a process to help both coach and teacher arrive at a focus for collaboration, a means of action, and a way of assessing whether the work accomplishes the intended objectives. It is a nonevaluative process that focuses on open-ended questions that elicit the teacher's responses while the coach remains a neutral partner.

Components of BDA

In Chapters 2, 3, and 4, we discuss each component of the BDA cycle in depth. Here is a brief description of the three elements:

- *Before*. The coach and the teacher explore the ideas, questions, issues, concerns, and challenges a teacher has with content, instructional delivery, or the class. Together they decide the focus of their work, the data they want to collect, and their respective roles during the specified classroom visitation.
- *During*. The coach and the teacher undertake their agreed-upon activities, roles, and tasks from the *before* session and take appropriate notes for later reflection and discussion. This is a data-collection process.
- *After*. The coach and the teacher share nonevaluative feedback and reflect on the goals, what they planned and implemented, what worked, and what adjustments are needed. The feedback is timely, intentional, and descriptive, resulting in changes in practice.

The BDA can serve as the primary mode of inquiry in both individual and group coaching situations. Although the cycle may be used to explore a single issue, its real objective is to help coaches, teachers, and school leaders become reflective practitioners and forge an ongoing collegial relationship built around strengthening practice across all content areas and with no planned or defined end.

The Importance of Confidentiality and Personalization

In our work we have found that effective instructional coaching as a professional development strategy is most likely to lead to professional learning when it is personalized—conducted one-on-one and in small groups. Certainly coaches can contribute their expertise in whole-school contexts, but teachers and school leaders gain the greatest benefits when coaching is practiced in more intimate settings. Think for a moment about private voice lessons. In which circumstance would a performer profit more: a group lesson where everyone gets the same attention or a private lesson where the performer's needs are the only needs addressed?

The Evidence Supporting Educator-Centered Instructional Coaching

Traditional in-service professional development does not serve teachers well. It is directed at groups of teachers, provided a few times during the school year with no follow-up or connection, and focused on generalized knowledge rather than the specific learning needs of individuals. In fact, there is a less than 5 percent chance of classroom application unless an instructional coach who practices with the teachers provides support (Joyce & Showers, 2002). This finding is also consistent with extensive literature indicating that one-on-one and small-group settings provide the circumstances most favorable and supportive of adult learning. Professional learning is about outcomes—what is learned, how deeply it is learned, and how well it is used in classrooms. Our framework is designed to ensure that what is learned through theory, demonstration, and practice is successfully implemented in the classroom (Cooper, n.d.; Joyce & Showers, 1988).

As this model began to be used more widely, we committed to conducting research to see if there was evidence that education-centered instructional coaching helped teachers and students. To that end, we designed and executed several studies asking whether, and in what ways, ECIC made any difference in schools and classrooms. We focused on the following:

- The impact of coached teachers on their students (student engagement and learning outcomes)

- The impact of instructional coaching on teachers (improvements in instructional practice)
- Whether and how coaches use the ECIC framework in their work

Student Outcomes

Standardized Test Results. For three years, we followed the experience of one elementary school in an economically disadvantaged Pennsylvania school district that adopted the ECIC model as a schoolwide approach to professional development. Teachers at all grade levels were coached. Our objective was to compare standardized test results over three years at this school with results at two other elementary schools with similar demographics that did not provide instructional coaching (Medrich, Fitzgerald, & Skomsvold, 2013).

As there was one coach working one-on-one and in small groups with all teachers at all grade levels, we were confident that everyone got the same quality of support and the same "basket" of individual, small-group, and schoolwide professional development experiences. Had there been more than one coach, our research might have been compromised by (possible) differences in the quality or nature of coaching provided by different coaches to different teachers.

With the help of school officials, we obtained standardized test results for each student at every grade level for a period of four years (encompassing the year before coaching began and the three years when teachers were being coached) for the school with coaching and two other schools. (Strict data security and anonymity protocols were employed, and all access to data was through an authorized third party.) Thus we were able to control for past performance of students before instructional coaching started at the school with coaching, as well as for the *expected* performance of each student at each of the three schools, based on prior actual performance, as modeled by the Pennsylvania Value-Added Assessment System (PVAAS, as described on the website of the Pennsylvania Department of Education—www.education.pa.gov).

Over the three years of study, students at most grade levels in the school with coaching made gains in standardized test performance at rates that exceeded their counterparts in the two control schools and that exceeded their expected performance as predicted by the PVAAS. Generally, students of teachers in the school with "wall-to-wall instructional coaching" were on a positive trajectory in reading (reversing a long-standing trend of poor performance at the school in the years before instructional coaching) at most grade levels, and the students showed gains that greatly exceeded those of their control-school counterparts.

The findings led us to a theory we continue to explore: *successful instructional coaching initiatives facilitate improvements in student learning over time*. In this case, over the three years, as teachers became comfortable with the coach and as the coach promoted an increasingly sophisticated professional development agenda, the school culture changed and the teachers changed their practices. The coach introduced teachers to new instructional practices, and in time, student learning improved. Equally important, as students passed from grade to grade and went from one coached teacher to another coached teacher, the students gained an additional advantage—they were exposed to consistently better quality of instruction.

Student Attendance. Another of our studies focused specifically on an important aspect of student engagement—attendance. This one-year study of four high schools looked at differences in student outcomes in one subject area for students of coached teachers as compared with students of teachers in the same school who were not coached. The most interesting finding was that, in looking class by class, students of coached teachers were far more likely to attend the class of their coached teacher as compared with students of teachers who were not coached, suggesting a significantly more attractive classroom climate. In related interviews, the principal confirmed that it was his observation over time that the coached teachers became better able to teach the curriculum in a way that engaged students (Medrich, 2013).

Teachers and Coaching

Our research has also identified some of the ways in which coaches are affecting teachers in classrooms. A survey (Medrich & Charner, 2007) of 2,000 teachers in 26 high schools with trained instructional coaches yielded the following data:

- Thirty-five percent were coached one-on-one at least once or twice a month.
- Seventy-seven percent of these one-on-one coached teachers said that the quality of their instruction improved.
- Eighty-one percent of the one-on-one coached teachers reported that their knowledge of research-based literacy strategies increased and deepened as a result of working with a coach.
- These teachers also became more involved in *other* professional development opportunities.
- Eighty percent said that their knowledge of research-based literacy strategies increased as a result of attending related professional development activities.

In addition—and most important—79 percent of one-on-one coached teachers self-reported that the quality of their instruction improved as a result of their involvement in these other professional development opportunities. The payoff came in terms of student engagement: 77 percent said their students were highly engaged during class.

A more recent survey of teachers in schools with coaching also demonstrated positive effects on student engagement and student learning (Charner & Mean, 2015):

- Ninety-two percent of teachers either received one-on-one coaching or participated in small-group or whole-school activities led by the coach. The teachers reported that coaching effectively addressed the BDA cycle of coaching as well as the essential elements of the PIIC framework most relevant to them: data analysis; intimate, personalized support from the coach; evidence-based literacy practices; and nonevaluative reflective practice.
- Eighty-four percent of these teachers reported changes in their classroom practice.
- Ninety-five percent of teachers who experienced a high level of one-on-one coaching *and* participated in coach-led small-group or whole-school professional development reported improvements in their classroom practice.

Even among those teachers who received only modest amounts of one-on-one coaching but participated in coach-led professional development, fully 84 percent reported changes in their instructional practice. Most important, nearly all of the teachers reported that the changes they made in their practice *had an impact on student learning, including improvements in students' ability to make connections to prior learning, deeper understanding of concepts, improvement in the quality of writing, and thinking more broadly about course material.*

Coaching Practice

As reported in one of our recent surveys of instructional coaches, most coaches use the elements and process of the ECIC framework and the BDA cycle of consultation in their day-to-day work (Charner & Mean, 2015). In addition, the survey found the following:

- Almost all of the coaches surveyed provided both one-on-one and small-group coaching to teachers.
- Close to 90 percent of the coaches surveyed used the BDA cycle of consultation and believed that they effectively addressed other essential elements of the coaching framework—literacy strategies, use of data, and applying nonevaluative reflective practice.

How Evaluation has Helped Us Improve Our Work

We use our research in several ways to support a continuous-improvement strategy—to help us refine and improve our model of instructional coaching. We use these data to arm our coaches with evidence that their work is, in fact, affecting how teachers teach and how students learn. This may seem obvious, but far from it; many who participate in initiatives like ours never have any sense of "how they are doing" or whether they are making a difference, or the evaluations become known only after the program has ended (in what is known as the autopsy report).

Our research indicates how instructional coaching has come to matter to teachers and students. And without question, our research has made a difference in terms of ensuring that our efforts are directed at improving the practice of instructional coaching as well as meeting the needs of schools, teachers, and students.

Summing Up

Coaching, already well recognized as a discipline in many professions, is slowly becoming part of the education lexicon. Educators are beginning to recognize that even though teachers are well educated, their practice can continuously improve through the "on the ground" support of instructional coaches. Coaches connect with teachers by respecting the processes that underlie adult learning. Our framework, with its three-step cycle of consultation, promotes coaching as a way of implementing and sustaining job-embedded, nonevaluative, personalized professional learning that empowers teachers. It provides multiple opportunities for colleagues to work together to use evidence-based strategies grounded in literacy to make a measurable difference in how they teach and how students learn. As documented by our research, educator-centered instructional coaching promotes professional learning, improves teacher instructional practice, and bolsters student engagement and student learning.

2

Part 1 of the BDA Cycle: The *B* — Planning

A vision without a plan is just a hallucination.

—Will Rogers

The before-during-after cycle of consultation and feedback is fundamental to our coaching framework, encompassing communication, collaboration, confidentiality, and collective problem solving. It enables coaches and teachers to work together to co-plan and co-design ways to enhance student learning, to visit classrooms after the planning and focus on a predetermined set of goals and objectives, and to reflect about what worked and if the goals and objectives for that lesson (or set of lessons) were met. It allows teachers to continually expand their knowledge base and work with trusted colleagues to make data-driven decisions that will yield changes in student learning.

Reviewing the BDA Components

As noted earlier, the starting point for the process is the *B*, or *before*, conversation. Here the coach and teacher co-plan and discuss the goals for the collaboration and how those goals will be achieved. The coach must be a good listener, asking probing or clarifying questions without giving opinions. The objective is for the coach to encourage the teacher to think about her goals, why they are important, and if the instruction and resources identified will address the students' needs. The coach's role during this phase is to help the teacher be metacognitive and generate her own ideas to support the intended outcomes. The teacher and the coach work together to construct the plan to collect evidence that will reflect the agreed-upon goals. At the *B* discussion, they also schedule a date to discuss what occurred during the classroom visit, giving themselves time to process what transpired in the classroom so that each partner has had an opportunity to reflect and craft questions on whether the goals for that session were met.

The *D*, or *during*, part of the cycle is the data-collection phase. The coach may visit the teacher's class and collect agreed-upon data, model a segment of the lesson, or co-teach with the teacher. Regardless of the activity, the *D* visit is evidentiary. It offers coach and teacher the information they need to reflect *on*, *in*, and *about* classroom practice. This is when they can literally see if what they wanted to do was accomplished. If the coach is actively teaching, the teacher is still responsible for collecting the data related to the items identified in the *before* phase.

The *A*, or *after*, part of the cycle is critical for transformation. This is when the coach and the teacher reflect and give timely, specific, descriptive, and nonjudgmental feedback to determine what worked and what practice, if any, needs additional support. This exchange does not happen on the same day as the actual visit because both parties need time to process what occurred in the classroom. Here the teacher and the coach consider what each might do differently the next time this content is taught or what instructional practice might be more effective to support this or other content. The *A* is a collective problem-solving session that often leads into the *before* of the next coach-teacher classroom collaboration. Across the BDA cycle, reflection and feedback are critical for changes in classroom practice and instruction.

BDA in Action

The BDA cycle of consultation can be applied in all kinds of relationships: coach-teacher; coach-mentor (coach's coach); and coach-principal. Its elements are both external (with teacher and coach reflecting together on practice) and internal (with coach and teacher reflecting individually on their own practice). The process is confidential, collaborative, conditional, and context-driven. Because the BDA cycle is situational, the coach facilitates, rather than dominates, the conversation, allowing the teacher's voice to be heard. It promotes an environment for collective problem solving where high expectations for effective instructional practices are the norm.

Consider the following case study, which details a problem of practice that we will follow through Chapter 4. Although this is just one example of a potential problem, it provides an opportunity to explore each segment of the BDA cycle in action alongside the teacher and coach.

Tackling Student Engagement:
Ellen's Journey with a Teacher

I once worked with a high school American history teacher who was having difficulty maintaining her students' focus in class. Students had little interest in the way she presented lessons, and they came to class unprepared, often late (if they came at all), and rarely inquisitive. She recognized that students were not engaged and that more of her time and energy were expended trying to maintain control rather than providing meaningful instruction.

She had no time to get help from other teachers during the busy school day, and she was uncomfortable admitting that she did not know what to do to improve the situation. It seemed to her that her teaching colleagues did not have the same challenges as she did. Although her principal had offered to work with any teacher looking for support, she did not want to go to the principal for fear of being labeled as marginal or deficient in her skills. The school also had me available as their instructional coach, but she was afraid that she would be labeled as "needy" if she sought my assistance.

After trying various strategies on her own—including new student groupings, changing her in-class test format, reducing homework to three days a week, and using more primary-source material in class—she recognized that these changes were not making a difference. Her students' attendance was still declining, few did homework, test scores were still low, and her students were not interested in improving their performance. She wanted to improve her skills but didn't know how.

The teacher finally asked me for help to understand what was happening and what she could do to engage her students and make their learning experience more meaningful. I was a veteran teacher and an experienced coach. I had worked extensively with individuals, small groups, and sometimes with the entire faculty on a number of issues as part of the school's regular professional development program. I knew this history teacher but had not worked with her. When she came to me, I was excited to collaborate with her through the BDA cycle of consultation.

As a coach, the first thing I needed to think about was how we would collaborate with consistency to stay focused on what she wanted to do and how she wanted to do it. As we began our conversation, I could tell that she was a bit unsure of how to answer my questions. Through our discussion, she recognized that her goals and what she wanted to do would guide the conversation. She realized that there was more than one way to approach her challenges and ongoing conversations about student work and engagement would help her define the changes she anticipated in this class and others. At one point she remarked, "All along, I felt that classroom management was the issue, but now I see that the more engaging and relevant my questions are to the tasks assigned to the students, the more attentive and engaged they will be in the lesson. If my assessments are tied to my goals, then that, too, will be more revealing about what my students know and are able to do when they leave my class." This "aha" moment was critical for change to take place. This teacher needed to understand what made the lesson relevant and how to engage her students every day. I was struck by her willingness to make intentional, bigger changes to her teaching strategies and methods rather than to just this lesson.

Deconstructing the *B* Phase

The *B* phase offers an opportunity for coach and teacher to get the conversation started, to step back and look at what they are trying to accomplish. Fostering dialogue is the basic unit of currency in the *B* phase. As Crane (2012) notes, "... it creates a pathway and a safety zone for an open conversation... [it] requires emotional safety for all participants; there must be no negative outcomes for expressing a point of view honestly and candidly" (p. 105). Easier said than done, and a challenge for both coach and teacher! Where and how you start pretty well determines how the process evolves and whether it meets the teacher's needs. So the dialogue that emerges during the *B* is a good indicator of the success of the *D* and the *A*.

During the *B* phase, the coach sets the stage but is all ears—helping the teacher formulate the "problem" they will work on together, asking questions that promote proactive thinking on the teacher's part, and helping the teacher think about her own beliefs and judgments. This is when the coach and the teacher collaborate about the goals and objectives of the lesson or unit plan (the subject of the BDA), identify instructional strategies and techniques that will help the students and teacher reach their goals, determine how the teacher will know if the students have accomplished the goals, decide how to address those students who have not, and select the most appropriate tools and other resources for the lesson. They co-construct the data that the coach will collect in the *D* visit and schedule a time to meet for the debriefing in the *A* meeting. In this phase of the cycle, the coach prepares by thinking about the following:

- *Description*. What questions will I ask so that the teacher can describe the lesson goals and purpose?
- *Envisioning*. How will the teacher's description help me envision what will happen during the class?
- *Self-assessment and reflection*. How will I know that the teacher is aware of how the lesson flows and where adjustments are needed?
- *Data collection*. What data should we collect that will provide feedback and information for the debriefing?

Description

It is essential to ask good questions and get ready to actively listen. Valuing teachers' voices and letting them guide the journey is important because they are the experts on their classroom and students, and listening to them creates a coach-teacher bond and empowers them to become leaders in their own right. Fostering a relationship based on collaboration, respect, and honor for the teacher's expertise wins teacher buy-in, which is essential for improved practice and student success.

Here are the kinds of questions that are critical in a *before* conversation:

1. What outcomes do you have in mind for your lesson? How do you envision your students will work collaboratively and meet the goals for the lesson? What formative assessments will you use to assess if your goals are being met? How often will you use this kind of assessment?
2. What concepts and skills are you addressing in your lesson? What in-class student tasks are directly related to the standards you are addressing?
3. How will you know that the students understand the content and are meeting the goals? What kind of homework assignments do you envision that demonstrate your students' understanding of the content? How will you review the homework and provide opportunities for revision?
4. What do you see yourself doing/asking to produce those student outcomes and elicit student responses that will meet the goals? What depth-of-knowledge questions will you ask that will extend your students' thinking and help them analyze the content?
5. How do you define active engagement? What self-assessment tools will you use to indicate a shift in approach is necessary? What primary-source materials are you planning to use that are relevant to the content? How do you envision

students making meaning of the text to demonstrate their understanding of the primary sources you plan to use?

6. What kind of feedback is important to collect that will help you determine if the lesson is successfully implemented? What kind of assessment for learning will you use to indicate what the students understand about the content?

7. What should we focus on as we co-construct the list of data to be collected during my visit? There are several effective instructional strategies that increase student engagement. Three of these are think/pair/share; sorting activities; and VIPs—very important points. How can you use these strategies to increase your students' interactions with the content and with each other?

Many of these questions, as well as those in Figure 2.1, get to the heart of what every teacher wants to do in class. The questions help coaches prepare for and differentiate their support for teachers. Remember, instructional coaching is not a cookie-cutter model. Coaches formulate questions around the teacher's specific goals and purpose. They engage teachers in conversations that honor their expertise, experience, voice, and choice. They help teachers envision the "what" and the "how" of ways to tackle their unique challenges. (Note: Figure 2.1 summarizes the kinds of questions that can be asked in the *before* session between the coach and the teacher. Please keep in mind that there are many similar questions that can be asked throughout the *before* conversation. Often one response leads to another thoughtful, probing question.)

Envisioning

Envisioning involves coach and teacher working together to brainstorm and articulate big ideas. The "Description" questions listed in the previous section can help them to set the tone for their interactions and do the following:

1. State the purpose of the coaching interaction—that is, what do you want to accomplish in this session?

2. Develop ways to translate the purpose into teacher and student actions and behaviors.

3. Identify benchmarks that demonstrate desired changes in student actions and behaviors.

4. Define the focus for data collection that will take place in the *D* (*during*) phase of the cycle.

Here it is worth repeating our emphasis on literacy as the foundation for all student learning. Early in our work with this model, we realized that literacy across all content areas was critical for student success. Regardless of the content, students needed to know how to interact with their texts and make meaning out of what they read. They needed to be surrounded by a literacy-rich environment guided by highly effective teachers who understood literacy learning and were able to differentiate their instruction for a diverse population. Whatever challenges teachers are facing or what goals they envision for their students, it will always be important to ensure that their classrooms are literacy-rich environments that promote questioning skills and effective group work using a variety of relevant texts.

Self-Assessment and Reflection

Donald Schön (1983) states that we need to reflect "in, on, and about" action. This model of coaching emphasizes ongoing opportunities for teachers to think about their thinking and their actions, how to contextualize their actions so they are aligned with their instructional plans, and how to make adjustments when the feedback suggests a need for change.

Questions are the currency of coaching, so asking rather than telling encourages teachers to think about their practices and creates the environment for teachers to take ownership of that thinking. Adults want to be the masters of their own learning and create their own agendas. Delivering someone else's agenda often misses the mark. With the help of a critical friend—aka the coach—teachers and coaches collaborate to plan, deliver, reflect, and adjust the teaching.

Helping teachers become more reflective practitioners is a critical goal for both coach and teacher. Coaches must reflect on the questions they ask; they must elicit the kinds of responses that lead to enhanced instructional practices and ultimately improve student learning. But they cannot stop there. They must also reflect on their own practices, the practices of the teachers they work with, and the continued professional development offered to support individual and collective schoolwide improvement endeavors.

Data Collection

The coach must prepare for the initial interaction with the teacher by thinking about the kinds of data to collect. This will help frame the conversations and help the coach and the teacher collaborate about goals, focus on strengths, and bolster the weaknesses in instructional practice. Ultimately, the coach needs to align the data collection and analysis to the application and utility of the collected data. These data help coaches understand the teacher they are working with and what they need to know about the teacher's goals. Two kinds of data are necessary to collect: school/demographic data and specific data about individual classrooms that

Figure 2.1 Questions for the *B* Phase

BEFORE The *before* is the planning phase, when the teacher and the coach collaborate and share the goals about instruction, co-create the data collection, and set a date and time for debriefing.	
Coach asks himself or herself these questions:	**Coach might ask the teacher these questions:**
Description (State the purpose of the lesson.) What goals, activities, materials, and design format are necessary to help achieve the goals of this lesson?	• What outcomes do you have in mind for your lesson today? • What do you want your students to know and be able to do when they leave your class? • What standards are you addressing in your lesson? • How will you know that the students understand the goals of the lesson?
Envisioning (Translate the lesson purposes into descriptions of desirable, observable student behaviors.) • What strategies/practices will I ask about or talk about that the teacher might use to meet the goals of the lesson? • What will student engagement look like during this lesson that the teacher and I can discuss? • What might I ask the teacher about meeting the expectations and goals of the lesson? • How will the teacher know that the goals were met? What if they were not? • How will I debrief this lesson?	• As you envision this lesson, what do you see yourself doing or asking to produce those student outcomes and elicit student responses? • What does active engagement look like in your class? • How will you know when differentiation is needed? • What challenges can you anticipate in this lesson? • How will you access your students' prior knowledge?
Self-Assessment and Reflection (Identify the benchmarks for determining student success.) • What will I ask the teacher about "taking the pulse" of the class? • How will I ask if the teacher and students are "on the same page"?	• How will you know that the students are engaged? • How will you know that they have met the goals? • What will you see students do or hear them say that indicates they understand the goals and directions for the lesson?
Data Collection (Depict the data-collecting role of the observer.) • What kinds of data can the teacher and I agree to collect that are important for this lesson?	• What do you want this lesson to accomplish? • What kind of feedback is important to collect that will help you determine the lesson's successful implementation? • What would you like me to focus on as we co-construct our data collection?

will help inform the coaching. Coaches can collect both quantitative and qualitative data, as illustrated in the following example.

Collecting Data

Schoolwide demographic data. After being hired as a coach in the school where I was already on staff, I decided that I needed to know more about the schoolwide strategic improvement plan and what each grade level/department indicated were their goals. I designed an online strategic notebook where I included what I knew about the school plans and invited a small group of teachers to add information that I had inadvertently missed and that they thought was important to include. That way, the teachers' voices could be heard about the kinds of things they thought we needed to collect in order to achieve our collective goals. I populated the strategic notebook with the school's mission statement and vision for improvement. Then I added a section about curriculum and program offerings, followed by information about after-school clubs and specialty-course opportunities for students. I knew that enrollment and student attendance data were important, but I didn't think about attendance data for staff, nor did I think about the graduation rates or promotion rates. These were all helpful additions suggested by the teachers that created wonderful opportunities for discussion and collaboration.

Interviews, surveys, and questionnaires. One of the things that was invaluable to me as a coach was interviewing teachers and other staff members about their perceptions of the school programs. I asked teachers from each department to describe the strengths of the programs offered, the roadblocks to student learning, and what professional development sessions would address their professional needs so they could work toward achieving the schoolwide improvement goals. Once I collected these data, I generated a survey asking for specific professional learning targets that were aligned to the goals. These surveys produced ideas that morphed into mini professional development sessions tied to teacher practices and offered monthly. Teachers collaborated with me, and together we provided a "menu" of professional development sessions that addressed teachers' needs so they could support their students' continued growth.

The *B* Phase in Action

Earlier in this chapter we introduced a case study related to Ellen's coaching of a history teacher. The following account describes the *B* phase of her work.

Ellen Sets the Stage

Because I was a coach on site, I already had a good grasp of the data about the school and student performance. I had thought about questions that would get to the heart of this American history teacher's thinking and foster a more metacognitive, thoughtful process about what a teacher wanted to teach, related planning for how to teach it, what the anticipated outcomes would be, and how that teacher would recognize when the goals were and were not met and adjust instruction to meet goals. That's what I call the "before the *before*" phase of the cycle, when I prepare my work before meeting the teacher for our planning session.

When we first met, we clarified her purpose: the teacher wanted to focus on student engagement and share nonfiction primary-source materials. She wanted students to "talk to their text" and summarize the important facts in the articles. She knew that her previous delivery modes had not yielded positive student outcomes, and she was willing to "step out of the box" to consider implementing new strategies. I opened the deeper discussion by asking the following questions:

- How do you feel your students' emotional well-being affects their capacity for learning?
- How do you think your students' past learning experiences influence their current ones?
- How do your students learn "best"?
- What kind of learner do you think *you* are? How do you learn best?
- What are the most effective learning experiences for you in your teaching practice?
- What do you think is the most conducive environment for learning?

Then, to understand what she understood about student learning, I needed to ask some questions about the differences between formative and summative assessments and the differences between assessment *of* and assessment *for* student learning. I needed to ensure that she knew how one type of assessment was the "diagnosis" (formative) and the other type was the "autopsy" (summative). We began by discussing what content the teacher wanted to explore and how she would help students understand it, and what she wanted them to be able to do once they left her class. We explored the difference between taking a "snapshot" of current learning and creating the "photo album" of what students should know and be able to do at the culmination of a unit of study. Through this conversation, she determined what about that content was important for students to know and how they would demonstrate their understanding. We also agreed that we would center our plans around reflection, feedback, and adjustments that would ensure that the content was well planned and implemented, materials and resources appropriate, and the assessments aligned with the curriculum. To get to this point, I asked these kinds of questions:

- How will you know that your students are fully engaged in the lesson?
- What might you hear students say and see them do that would indicate they are "on task" and understand the directions for their tasks?
- How will you know when you need to make adjustments in your instructional delivery?

I also tried to find out about some details about the content she planned to teach and how she planned to make it engaging, using these questions:

- What topic do you want to focus on in today's lesson? Do students have the right level of mastery and a literacy-rich environment that equips them with what they need to reach your goals for the lesson?
- What do you want students to know and be able to do by the end of the class *and* by the end of the unit? How will you know that they clearly understand your expectations and goals?
- What kinds of activities are appropriate for reaching the lesson's goals? Why?
- How will students connect their previous learning with this new learning?
- How will you know when students are fully engaged? How will you help those who are not?

We discussed all of these questions at length. She struggled to clarify goals for her students, so together we brainstormed a couple of strategies: (1) sentence strips on the board that clearly indicated the lesson topic, goals, and expectations for the day; the strips could be posted around the room to provide a running account of each unit's goals throughout the year; (2) organizing students into groups, with each group selecting a leader and a time keeper. Once the goals and directions were shared as a whole class, each leader reviewed the goals and directions in the group and asked for clarifying questions to manage the tasks. I underlined how important a literacy-rich classroom environment was to making these strategies work.

Lesson design was a huge factor in student engagement and classroom management. We explored how her students interacted with each other and how they completed their tasks. She had some "moving" parts to the lesson—for example, station rotation, distribution of primary source materials, partnering, and so on—so we reviewed the time it took for students to move, how the materials were disseminated and collected, how the social groupings were organized to ensure active learning (such as putting frequently absent students and disengaged students with more-engaged peers to encourage participation), and the pace and flow of the lesson. Aside from questions about setup, we also discussed strategies for maintaining an organized and seamless pace, such as walking around the room and sitting with each group for brief periods, or ways of including students in formative assessment, to "take the pulse." And because she had special concerns about why the students in the back of the room tended to be more off task and disengaged, we decided to collect data about whom the teacher called on when asking questions.

To think of some additional *Look Fors* on which to base data collection, we designed a T-chart indicating what a classroom with students on task looks like and sounds like. For instance, we agreed that students who are actively engaged in their tasks talk about the topic and what they need to complete the assignments; they look at one another and their papers, projects, and writing assignments; they help each other by asking clarifying and probing questions; they collaborate to find out information appropriate to the topic; they disagree without being disagreeable; they respect each other's thoughts and want to know more about what they are learning; they experience "accountable talk" focusing on achieving the goals of the lesson. We determined that the following measurable *Look Fors* would constitute the most relevant data to collect in the *D* (*during*) phase:

- How many students have their homework on this particular day?
- During group work, how many students are working together and how many are sitting back and waiting for the answers? What are the unengaged students doing?

- What materials and resources are used? Are they grade-level appropriate and content appropriate? Do these materials support the goals?
- Does the teacher go around the room and sit at different tables to keep the pulse of the class?
- How does the teacher move from activity to activity? Is there enough time for the movement or too much time? Does the teacher ask questions without giving students time to think about their answers or share their thoughts with their peers?
- Does the teacher "cover" material without giving students time to process the learning or reflect on the learning?

Here we briefly interrupt Ellen's account to offer a few observations. By working with a coach to help shape thinking, the teacher is able to discuss, practice, and rehearse the actual content before getting in front of the students. The kinds of questions Ellen asked can be used to initiate any BDA cycle. They are at once general and specific. The objective is that through the coach's questioning skills, the teacher will become more reflective and recognize alternatives that will improve classroom results. If the teacher's intended outcomes or goals are flawed, then the instructional practices won't ensure meaningful student engagement. The important point is that the questioning process promotes dialogue and introspection in the planning stage. Now we return to Ellen's account.

Time is needed to process the discussion following the *B* conversation. The history teacher and I shared information central to establishing a partnership and conducting the cycle of consultation. In that crucial meeting, I got a better understanding of the teacher, her style, and her view of teaching and learning and the issue at hand. Through the process, she also got the opportunity to think about how she would like to work with me. Together, we decided on a date for the *D* phase and a date for the *A* meeting. The stage was set.

Summing Up

The BDA cycle of coaching is critical to all coaching interactions. Figure 2.1 provides a summary of the general questions that coaches should ask themselves and those that they should ask the teacher in the *B* phase of the BDA cycle. The conversations that occur in the *before* sessions are deliberate and intentional, designed to identify goals and to co-construct the data collection tool. Setting goals early on, visualizing how those goals will be actualized, deciding which data to collect, and identifying the ways to assess which practices were effective and which need to be strengthened set the tone for the coaching interaction. Without the benefit of planning and preparation, the conversations will be unfocused and the purpose unclear, making the coaching conversations ineffective as a way to help teachers improve and refine their practice.

3

Part 2 of the BDA Cycle:
The *D* — Visiting and Modeling

The coach who models provides a visual example that often helps teachers reach an "aha" moment. Modeling is helpful when a practice is new to teachers, when they are not certain of how to implement a specific strategy; when teachers are unsure of whether 'it' will work for their students; or when teachers are having specific difficulties with implementation.

—Rita M. Bean and Jacy Ippolito, *Cultivating Coaching Mindsets*

Because teachers are used to being evaluated by administrators who observe, take a "snapshot," and offer limited advice relative to their observation, teachers may not see the coach as someone who can genuinely contribute to their professional growth. Additionally, most teachers are accustomed to working in isolation. The possibility of talking with a coach about practice and having someone other than an administrator visit a class may be uncomfortable for anyone not experienced in sharing the planning and delivery of instruction. Coaches need to be able to show teachers that classroom visits can help strengthen practice. Accomplishing this can be a real challenge, especially because the coach's visit is nonevaluative, whereas the administrator's observation is designed to evaluate the teacher's performance.

Every teacher experiences classroom challenges regardless of years of service, school setting, or content knowledge. In the case study of the high school American history teacher introduced in Chapter 2, it took some time for the teacher to feel comfortable enough to seek support from the coach. She didn't want to be viewed as someone who needed help. However, after recognizing she needed to do something different in her classroom, she acknowledged that the coach might be able to help and found the courage to contact her. This was not an easy decision. First, she had to dismiss her preconceived notion that coaches worked only with poorly skilled teachers and accept that coaching was not a deficit model. At the same time, the coach had to understand that the teacher's interpretation of teachers and coaches working together might get in the way of their collaboration. Here's how their relationship evolved.

Ellen's Journey, Continued

After careful and deliberate planning in part *B* of the cycle, the teacher and I were both aware of our roles in the classroom visitation—the *D*, or *during*, phase. In the *B* meeting, I was very clear that I would remain focused solely on the co-constructed goals for the *D* visit. I knew that I was going to notice other things during class that I would be tempted to comment on or question, but I would have to remember to only ask questions and gather data about the things on which she and I had agreed. Of course, this could prove challenging. A few scenarios entered my mind: What if I catch some glaring content errors? What if I see some ineffective teacher behaviors that were not originally discussed? What if the teacher forgets to bring materials and begins to search around for the handouts she planned to use? Should I intervene and help keep the students on track while she roots through her box of materials? What if students take out their smartphones and begin listening to music while the teacher is trying to review the work? Should I unobtrusively approach those students and tell them to put their phones away?

Lesson learned: I thought back to once when, as a new coach with the best of intentions, I deviated slightly from my plans with a teacher to collect data and briefly reminded some students who were distracted by their phones to put them away. Because we decided that one of the goals was student engagement, I felt confident that my intervention was necessary. In retrospect, I should have followed our agreed-upon plan and simply asked questions in the *A* (*after*) meeting to let the teacher come to her own conclusions about the cause of the issue and next steps to address it. I took that lesson with me into the *D* phase with this history teacher.

Conducting the *D*

The *during* phase of the BDA cycle can proceed in different ways: the teacher may teach while the coach watches, listens, and takes notes; or the coach may teach while the teacher watches, listens, and takes notes; or they may co-teach in a joint effort to achieve the lesson's goals. Often the teacher and the coach have discussed some strategies that the teacher would like to see implemented by the coach or that the teacher would like to try in a nonevaluative setting to get beneficial feedback. Depending on the roles taken, the coach or teacher (or both) collect data and then reflect separately before they get together to debrief at the *after* meeting. Having this time to process the experience and generate some questions about what they each saw provides additional content for the debriefing. The coach or the teacher may see something that was unexpected and want to return to that without abrogating the *before* agreement (ensuring that the data gathered are the agreed-upon data). The teacher should always be welcome to discuss something new, but coaches need to remain circumspect, particularly in the beginning. Until the relationship is fully developed, with good rapport, the coach needs to be sensitive to the teacher's emotion. The coach can eventually push the teacher to nurture growth, but only after they have established trust and are comfortable admitting what they don't know and working together to learn new things. The following sections present some things to keep in mind as you proceed through the *D* phase.

When the Teacher is Teaching

In this situation, the coach stays to the side and focuses on what the students and teacher say and do specifically as it relates to the identified goals for the lesson. The coach asks, "What are students doing during the class? Are they engaged in accountable talk—that is, are they talking about the assigned tasks and are they working toward achieving the lesson goals?

The coach remains objective and nonevaluative when taking notes and comments only on the behaviors and actions that are related to the goals for the lesson that were agreed upon in the *B* meeting. The focus is strictly on collecting evidence that speaks to student and teacher behaviors and not on giving an opinion on whether or not the actions, words, and behaviors support accomplishing the goals.

One useful tool to use when collecting data is a T-chart with two columns: one for what the teacher says and does, and one for what the students say and do throughout the lesson. This is a report, not a reflection. No value judgments or appraisals are included on this chart; only the documentation of actual events, statements, and actions. Here's how Ellen went about the process.

Ellen Begins Collecting Data

The history teacher and I had agreed upon a co-teaching approach. As I took notes in class during the *D* phase, I thought about the following questions:

- How does this content relate to the goals?
- What kinds of questions does the teacher ask? What higher-order questions that require students to think deeply about their answers are asked?
- How are students expected to collaborate with one another during this class? Do they understand how to collaborate as well as cooperate?
- What signals do the students "send" to show they are off task and disengaged?
- Does the teacher notice that students are off task? What does she do and say to bring students back on task?

I based my answers on the data we had agreed to collect in the *B* phase:

- How many students have their homework on this particular day?
- Were goals made clear? Does the teacher use the sentence strips we discussed?
- During group work, how many students are working together and how many are sitting back and waiting for the answers? What are the unengaged students doing?
- What materials and resources are used? Are they grade-level appropriate and content appropriate? Do these materials support the goals?
- Does the teacher go around the room and sit at different tables to keep the pulse of the class?
- How does the teacher move from activity to activity? Is there enough time for the movement or too much time? Does the teacher ask questions without giving students time to think about their answers or share their thoughts with their peers?
- Does the teacher "cover" material without giving students time to process the learning or reflect on the learning?
- Does this class, overall, resemble the T-chart that we co-designed in the *B* meeting?

I took notes using a pen and paper rather than an iPad or other portable device. (I had learned through experience that using portable devices was often associated with administrative observations, clearly a different event than a classroom visitation.)

While collecting the data, I noticed that the students in the back of the room were talking to each other. I asked myself the following questions:

- What are the students talking about? Are they questioning each other about the content or assigned tasks?
- Is student inquiry about content driving the class? Are their responses relevant to the lesson or are they trying to move the class and teacher off task?
- Are the students in the process of completing one activity while the teacher is moving on to the next one?
- Are the students confused about the directions and tasks they are assigned to complete?
- What changes in student behavior would occur if students had an opportunity to work together to complete the tasks?

I also noticed that the students interrupted several times to ask questions that were not related to the class. For instance, one student asked if the pep rally at the end of the week would be on the field or in the gymnasium. Another student then called out that she was going to bring her friend from another school. A third student asked if the cheerleaders were planning to cheer or only the drum majorettes would be performing. Instead of reminding students that these questions were immaterial to the lesson, the teacher answered the first question and, of course, had nothing to say about the following two comments except to try to talk over the ensuing conversation, which was not effective.

I made a note of these so the two of us could discuss these interruptions as an indicator of student disinterest and lack of engagement, which we had agreed would be the focus when we met for our planning (B) session. For instance, one agreed-upon example of a data collection point for student engagement could be noting whom the teacher calls on for answers. If the teacher calls on only the "first row" students or those in a specific group, the others may become discouraged from raising their hands or completing assignments because they know the teacher will not call on them.

As I sat watching the students work while the teacher was teaching, I saw that there were really only 3 or 4 students out of 25 who were the leaders in the class—that is, *disruptive* leaders. The other students were quiet and on task. They did, however, watch the teacher and wait for her responses to the disruptions. To reclaim the class, I knew something had to be done quickly and painlessly. I didn't want the students calling out "You are not our teacher" if I intervened, or equally embarrassing, "Why can't you be our teacher?"

Being a teacher or a coach means that decisions "in, on, and about" action need to occur immediately. I decided to move swiftly and not give any student an opportunity to make a comment. Instead of targeting the disruptive students, which would cause everyone to focus on me, I moved quickly to the students who were on task, asking if they needed any help to complete the task. Because they were in pairs, I quietly suggested that they share their work with each other and check for understanding and clarity. If they had any questions, they could ask each other now rather than wait until their teacher was finished with the disruptive students. I shared the "Ask three before me" technique, to which they seemed to respond by turning to their partners with questions or comments.

On rare occasions, a teacher may not want a coach to take notes. In such cases, the coach must be understanding and comply. This is difficult because a coach's actions are dependent upon the teacher's actions. The coach's practice is defined by the needs of the teacher. Not collecting the agreed-upon data makes it difficult to plan the next steps.

One way to address this kind of issue is to have an open and honest conversation in the planning (*before*) phase. Here, the coach shares her responsibilities in the coaching practice and process with the teacher and helps the teacher understand that taking notes (only on the agreed-upon items) is the basis for the debriefing and identifying where changes in practice are necessary. Without notes, a coach cannot help the teacher plan next steps. One way to maintain total transparency is to offer to give the notes to the teacher at the end of the visit and ask the teacher to bring them to the debriefing (*after*) session.

When the Coach is Teaching

In this situation, the teacher stays on the side and focuses on what the students and the coach say and do. The teacher collects specific data related to the goals of the lesson as discussed in the *before* session.

Ellen's Journey with the History Teacher, Continued

In the *before* phase, the teacher and I agreed on each of our roles in the co-teaching approach. When it was my turn to teach the class, my goal was for the teacher to notice how and what I did to promote student engagement and collaboration. I wanted her to record how I clarified goals of the lesson, what I asked, how long I waited for student responses, how I transitioned from one activity to another, and what I did when students were not on task. I wanted her to focus on when I realized the students were not on task and how I brought them back to the instructional moment. I wanted her to be able to reflect on questions like these:

- What are the students saying and doing while I am teaching this segment of the lesson?
- How do I respond to students who are off task? What do I say to them? Where am I standing?
- How do I help students work with one another?
- How do I move around the classroom, keeping my eyes on the students and what they are doing?
- Are the materials placed so that I can get to them easily?
- Do the students have resources or do I distribute them during class? If I distribute resources, what is the method of distribution?

I wanted the teacher to ask me about my words and actions so that we could discuss the ways in which the students were engaged and what I did to encourage that engagement or discourage the apathy.

She recorded her observations on the T-chart. On one side of a two-column sheet she wrote down the actions or what she heard; on the other side, she wrote probing questions or clarifying comments so that she could ask me to explain the thinking behind my actions when we debriefed in our *A* meeting. The process focused on metacognitive behavior, with the coach modeling how thinking about action is a deliberate and intentional practice.

Coaches collect a lot of data and then organize the talking points according to the agreed-upon items decided in the *before* session. Those are the items the coach and the teacher reflect on in the *after* session. If an issue emerges that is not one of the agreed-upon items, the coach may shift gears and move toward scheduling the next *before* phase of the BDA cycle with the new issue setting the context for that discussion. Or the coach may ask the teacher something like this: "So, when you wanted me to collect data on student engagement, I noticed that some students were very involved and eager to participate. They were the students that you called on quite frequently. Why do you think those students participated throughout the class while some, especially those in the back of the room, were not fully engaged?" The objective in the *after* session is to revisit the goals identified in the *before* session and reflect on what was accomplished in the *during* session. These sessions need to be aligned.

Summing Up

The *during* phase is when the coach and the teacher can see how their planning and practice are actualized. Figure 3.1 provides a summary of the general questions that coaches should ask themselves and those that they should ask the teacher in this part of the BDA cycle. As the case study and examples demonstrate, in actual practice the general questions are adapted to tackle a multitude of specific issues. The questions guide coaches as they work to open conversations with both teachers and school leaders and are truly "conversation starters."

The key point to remember is that a well-planned lesson is only as effective as the delivery, and seeing the delivery in person is essential. Without a classroom visitation in the *D* phase, a joint reflection and debriefing session is not possible, because the coach would only "hear" about the class events through the teacher's filter. That account becomes a one-sided description or report rather than actual data collection from another person in the room. Although data collection is not the only critical part of the process, it is the part that forms the structure and substance of the debriefing and feedback process in the *A* phase that follows.

Figure 3.1 Questions for the *D* Phase

DURING	
In the *during* phase, the coach and the teacher decide on their respective roles. Together, they decide if the coach will collect data, model a portion of the class, or co-teach with the teacher.	
Coach asks himself or herself these questions:	**Coach might ask the teacher these questions:**
Metacognition (Help teacher monitor his or her own thinking during the lesson.) • What will I ask the teacher about students meeting the expectations of the class? • What will I ask the teacher so he or she is fully aware of when shifting is necessary? How will I know that shifting is necessary?	• Does this lesson support your goals for the day? • What signals indicated that students were not on track and the lesson was not proceeding as planned? • What were you thinking when you decided to change the design of the lesson? • How did you try to steer the lesson back on course? What would have helped make the shift flow more smoothly?
Infer from Data (Draw hypotheses and explanations from the data provided.) • Does the teacher understand formative assessment? • What does the teacher need to know about the data? • What should the teacher ask himself or herself about the data? • How can I help the teacher understand that the data may be "in the moment"?	• What ongoing formative assessment data will you collect during the class? • What can you infer about your students and the data collected? • What data were the most significant to meeting the goals of your lesson? • How did you pace your lesson to ensure all students understood the content?
Inquiry (Help teacher make the lesson more inquiry based.) • What do I need to know about inquiry to help the teacher understand it? • How do I help teachers ask appropriate-level questions?	• What did the students say? • What can you learn from the students' responses? • Were the students actively engaged in questioning each other about content? • Did student inquiry drive the class? • What, if anything, got in the way of the lesson?

Source: From *Cognitive Coaching: Developing Self-Directed Leaders and Learners* (3rd ed.), by Arthur L. Costa and Robert J. Garmston, 2016, Lanham, MD: Rowman & Littlefield, pp. 329–331. Copyright 2016 by Rowman & Littlefield. Adapted with permission.

4

Part 3 of the BDA Cycle: The A — Reflecting and Debriefing

> *By three methods we may learn wisdom: First, by reflection, which is noblest; second, by imitation, which is easiest; and third, by experience, which is the bitterest.*
>
> —Confucius

So, here we are at what Confucius calls the "noblest" part of learning—reflective practice. Why is reflection so important? It is the process by which we think about *what happened.* In instructional coaching, this reflective practice takes place when coaches give teachers the opportunity to reflect internally and externally in nonevaluative surroundings. Coaches strive to make the authentic and meaningful collaborative conversations a habit so that teachers—and coaches themselves—consider how they think and act, which deepens their knowledge, expands their skills, and applies their new learnings to accomplish their goals. Reflection is a metacognitive process that helps teachers and coaches focus on the "why" rather than the "what."

Effective teachers reflect in, on, and about practice continually. Reflection is the mindful consideration of one's professional actions, "a challenging, focused, and critical assessment of one's own behavior as a means towards developing one's own craftsmanship" (Osterman, 1990, pp. 133–152). It is a "dialogue of thinking and doing through which [one] becomes more skillful" (Schön, 1987, p. 31). It is not a report documenting an action but rather a revelation about the thinking process and what was learned from the experience; it is the rationale behind the actions and the learning that guides next steps. Without reflection, there is no thought-provoking dialogue (or monologue) that results in adjustments to teaching in either content or process.

The following kinds of questions help coaches prepare for the nonevaluative debriefing in the *A* session:

- What questions will I ask myself to assess how the lesson progressed? How will I tie my questions to the agreed-upon *Look Fors*? What will I say if the lesson did not go as expected? How will I help the teacher assess her own understanding of what happened in class and use that data to make changes in her class structure?
- What kinds of questions will I ask her to recall about what the students said and did? How will I help her relate her understanding of student engagement to student performance? How will I know that she understands student engagement? How will I ask her if she knows what got in the way of student learning?
- How can we compare performance of students who were engaged and those who were not engaged? How did what the teacher saw me do and say compare with what she did and said?
- What conclusions can we both draw about our independent and collective practices? Which instructional practices seemed to work more effectively than others in keeping students on track?
- During the debriefing session, how will I help the teacher be reflective and transparent? What will I ask her so she can self-assess her practice? Is my feedback timely, nonjudgmental, targeted, intentional, and tied to our goals and classroom practices?
- How am I assessing my own practice, and what do I need to change as I move forward with this teacher?

These are not the only questions that the coach can prepare for the debriefing session; however, they are generic and applicable to each time the teacher and coach meet. They form the basis of the feedback conversation and can be used as a self-assessment tool for coaches. It is important for coaches to ask questions that get to the heart of the reflection and instigate changes where needed. Asking the right questions is critical for the feedback loop.

What's interesting about the debriefing is that the feedback given and received here is what makes a difference in the transformation of teaching and the student outcomes. This is when positive and supportive conversations take place, supported by analysis and in-depth inquiry; the thinking is challenged and the rationale for instructional delivery is exposed and explained.

Relationships: The Key to Successful Reflection

Neither new coaches nor school staff are always ready to jump in and facilitate reflective, one-on-one conversations. It takes time to develop the kinds of relationships needed to form the foundation for such conversations. Knowing, however, that reflection must take place in order to change practice, many new coaches try another, subtler approach and generate their more personalized coaching interactions via a small-group learning cohort. This is very effective in schools where professional learning communities (PLCs) are already established and the individual communities focus their attention on specific goals, topics, book studies, grade-level content, and similar matters. The coach can easily work with individual learning communities and begin the BDA cycle of consultation with them as a group working on a common theme. Doing so removes the pressure of one-on-one conversations until both parties feel comfortable enough to connect that way. When working with such groups, it is important to determine the kinds of PLCs the school has established and what their goals are, and to learn as much as possible about the group itself. It's always preferable to start coaching interactions with some kind of schoolwide data as an access point and to reflect on those data to determine successful implementation. With these points in mind, let's return to Ellen's coaching experience.

....

Ellen's Journey, Continued

Today, as a coach, I meet with teachers and we discuss various ideas that go far beyond "covering" topics and keeping students in their seats. We engage in a recursive process in which coaching interactions are multiple, differentiated, and structured but not evaluative or threatening. The teachers expect our collaboration to be reciprocal and seamless; we work together to discuss, plan, practice, and debrief to create teaching and learning moments consistently, regularly, and purposefully through the entire BDA cycle.

But my practice didn't start this way; it had to be built. Once I became familiar with the teachers and built awareness with the staff about the instructional coaching model, I was able to establish relationships and help them collaborate with each other. In the beginning, I didn't focus on meeting one-on-one; I concentrated on building my coaching credibility by co-facilitating professional development sessions with my teaching colleagues and then branching out to create more meaningful conversations that turned the professional development into professional learning. That is, I targeted the areas for improvement that the teachers suggested were important, provided some mini professional development sessions around those topics, and followed up with more direct conversations to discuss how well the teachers learned the concepts and were able to apply them across their content areas. These were all part of the BDA cycle of consultation with small groups rather than one-on-one. I was not quite ready for the one-on-one conversations with the faculty "at large."

In *before* sessions, as a group we described and envisioned what we wanted to do collectively and independently. We assessed where we were and then made adjustments to our actions based on our collective thoughts and ongoing conversations. In the *during* sessions, we focused on our goals and the plans to ensure that we met our goals; at the same time, we discussed what kind of data we should collect to inform our thinking and instructional decisions. In the *during* phase, we provided professional development sessions that were organic; that is, they grew out of continuing conversations with the staff. My teaching colleagues were willing to co-facilitate some sessions and did so with the understanding that we would talk to the staff afterward to see if we had met our intended outcomes. Although the *B* and *D* phases were critical, the open, nonevaluative, and private *A* (*after*) sessions were where we explored lines of inquiry together that helped us reflect and determine which instructional practices were strong, which needed strengthening, and which needed to be replaced. This created the next step in changing thinking and talking about effective practice.

Meanwhile, the American history teacher and I made some great strides in promoting text rendering, talking to the text, and making meaning from the text; developing a mutual understanding of what was important from the text; and brainstorming what strategies the teacher would use to elicit the students' understanding of the text, to assess whether the students understood the VIPs (very important points) of the text, and to look for indicators that the teacher needed to adjust her teaching when she noticed that the students were not fully involved. We achieved this through a number of BDA cycles that included some intense reflection in our *A* meetings. The first *A* meeting was the most delicate one, but we made significant headway. Here is how we did it.

Based on the dialogue between the teacher and me, her knowledge of the problem of practice, and the classroom visitation, I began preparing for our first *A* meeting by asking myself two "internal" questions to ensure that

the conversation focused on the goals and ideas expressed in the *before* conversation and aligned with what happened in the *during* class session:

1. *What kind of evidence did I collect about the students' actions, the teacher's actions, and my own actions?* When I asked myself this question, I
   remembered that in our *before* meeting, this teacher wanted to focus
   on increasing student engagement and using more techniques that
   would help students become involved in the lesson. She realized that
   the struggles she had with classroom management were really related
   to her lesson design. Her students were not involved, not motivated,
   and were often unprepared.

We started by talking about expectations and what she wanted to
see in class and strategies for clarifying goals and expectations, including
checking for understanding; we talked about what an effective classroom
environment looked like and how she would know that her students were
engaged. We also discussed strategies to ensure engagement, such as grouping more-engaged students with less-engaged students and moving through
the classroom, periodically sitting at different tables with students, to keep
a constant "pulse" of the class. We designed a T-chart to describe what we
thought an engaged class would look like.

In my initial *before* meeting, I asked the teacher if I could take notes. She
agreed, so in the D session I took notes on a two-column sheet, and she did
the same when I was teaching. That way, I could write my own questions
about what the teacher and the students said and did. I wanted to have
these notes so that I could compare what I saw with what was planned. I
asked her to use the same form when I taught my segment so we could talk
about my actions as well.

2. *Were my planned questions thought-provoking, helping the teacher to arrive
   at her own conclusions?* I reminded myself that questioning is critical
   in the coaching process. I needed to ask questions that would eventually lead the teacher to "aha" moments. I would know that my questions were provocative and stimulating if they became a springboard
   for ensuing conversations, open ended rather than one-size-fits-all.

In our first *after* meeting, we discussed what we saw or heard, making
sure that all statements were evidence-based and the opinions were formed
as questions with all elements aligned to focuses we had agreed to in the
before. I made sure to pace the conversation to give us both time to review
and reflect on the goals and outcomes of the lesson. The feedback loop was
reciprocal; in this case, we both held the role of teacher and data collector,

so we were both able to give and receive specific, nonjudgmental feedback. Here is how the conversation unfolded:

- *What did you recall most about your students during this class? How did the students respond to the lesson? How do you know they understood the goals, directions, and focus of the lesson? How did you assess their learning?*

Her response: I thought we started out with clear directions because no one asked any questions. I wrote the goals on the board using sentence strips and read them aloud, so I thought the students knew what we planned to do. I noticed, however, that some students didn't have their notebooks out and were searching in their book bags when I reviewed the goals. Other students were looking at me and the board so I thought they were following along. Maybe I should have waited until everyone was ready before I started talking.

- *As you reflect on your lesson, what are your perceptions about student engagement, behavior, activity transitions, and lesson pace? How can you compare what you planned to the actual outcomes of the lesson?*

Her response: I thought what I planned to cover was appropriate. When the students looked at me talking, I thought they were following along. As I think back, just looking at me really didn't mean they were "with" me. I could tell that the students in the back of the room were doing other things, but I was afraid to move to the back because then I would lose the students in the front who responded to my questions. I now realize that the students in the back were really not engaged and that gave them the opportunity to get distracted and off task.

When I noticed more students were fidgeting, I just went faster and moved the conversation along. Unfortunately, looking back, I know that there was no conversation. I asked questions and the few students in the front answered them, and then we just moved forward with the next step of questions/content I included in my plans. I think there was quite a disparity between what I wanted to see and what I actually saw.

- *What evidence did you see that indicates your goals were met? What conclusions can you draw about their learning for the day? What got in the way of some students reaching the goals you intended?*

Her response: Even though we planned together and talked about the goals and collecting evidence, I was distracted and nervous and wanted to keep moving. I thought the faster I moved, the better chance I would have for the students to move with me. The evidence, however, suggests that some students "got" it and most did not. The students in the front and a few sprinkled through the class understood and were able to answer questions and respond to me. But I really did not engage the others. I know that because they didn't answer my questions. I wonder though… does that mean they didn't understand the content or they didn't understand what I asked? Maybe they understood the content but were uninterested in showing what they understood. I think my desire to move the content along without really assessing what the students understood got in the way of their learning. I moved but they didn't.

- *What would make this lesson more effective?*

Her response: We talked about moving around the room and partnering more-engaged with less-engaged students so that they could talk to each other and then feel more confident about answering questions. When I saw you do that, I realized that the students needed the opportunity to talk and learn together; that maybe checking with each other first was what they needed to feel more comfortable about understanding the content. I don't think I waited long enough for students to respond, nor did I give them an opportunity to think about their answers before I called on someone I knew had the answer.

The pacing was also an issue. I didn't go around the room and join students at tables as much as I had planned, and I don't think I gave them enough time to show their mastery of the content. If I had waited more for students to show that they either understood or didn't understand the question, asked them to turn to their partners and discuss their thoughts and then share, that would have made quite a difference. They would not be afraid that their answer was wrong because their partner probably agreed with them.

I need to give more time for students to think about the content. And I need to ask different kinds of questions, probably more about analysis or comparisons to encourage higher-order thinking rather than just recall.

- *Is there a difference between the students' performance and your intended outcomes?*

Her response: Since we collaborated on the planning, I knew the expectations. But I also knew that I had trouble engaging students and tapping into their bank of knowledge. They kept getting distracted, asking about the pep rally. In a way, the outcomes of content were different because the students could not demonstrate their knowledge, which I hoped they could, but I was not surprised that I still had trouble engaging them since this happens frequently. The difference I noticed was the way you handled the lack of interest and how you moved the students to a more comfortable "place" to discuss and share with their partners. It seemed like you were not worried that the students had too much time to think; you gave them the time they needed and didn't worry about the next set of questions you wanted to ask.

- *In which activities during this lesson did the students participate the most? Why?*

Her response: I thought the students participated more when they were partnered and asked to read the section a few times and then share with their partners the way you and I decided to facilitate. Checking at each time they read for a different purpose before moving on to the next activity was quite effective. You made sure the students understood the task and completed it before moving forward. I think they felt more comfortable knowing that someone else shared the same ideas, the difficulty with unknown words, and unclear or confusing content. Watching the students interact with each other allowed me to sit back and see which students really did understand the content and goals and which needed more support. You were not doing all the talking, and that was something I never thought about trying.

- *If you were to evaluate the effectiveness of the lesson format, instructional delivery, content, and student outcomes, what would you do differently the next time you teach these students?*

Her response: First of all, thank you for collaborating with me and helping me think through my ideas and how I would accomplish them. I would definitely build into each lesson time for students to think about what I asked them and to share with their partners. I may assign different partners as we move forward so they don't get *too* comfortable, but I would definitely use this technique regularly. The other thing I would work on is the wait time. I need to remember that thinking does take time and that I need to wait until everyone is settled before I start giving directions.

I wonder if I could ask the students what they think is important in certain sections of their text. Then they could share what they think is important, the VIPs you talked about, and then move forward from there. I think I could move toward implementing that strategy, but I'm not there yet. If I can do these things, I think the next lesson will look at lot more like the T-chart that we designed in the *B* meeting.

- *What do you think motivated your decisions throughout the class?*

Her response: I'm not really sure. I think it may have something to do with being the first time a coach visited me. I think I also wanted to make sure that I had time to implement all of the new strategies we discussed, so I rushed through the work. I'm going to have to think about that some more.

- *Self-reflection is critical, and it can be tricky. I'm glad you're going to think more about this. When you begin the reflective process, think about your own interactions with your family or friends. What happens when you think about multiple ways to address an issue? Different perspectives create other ways to look at the same issues. How would your teaching strategies change if you always asked yourself the question, "How will this help increase student engagement?"*

Her response: Good idea! I will try that today. From now on, I'll work on tying how each of my professional decisions in the classroom will help improve student engagement and learning.

I was very glad to learn that the teacher then had some questions for me about my practice in front of the class: *Why did you stop when you noticed students were becoming distracted? When did you realize that students did not understand the directions? What made you decide to steer the lesson in a different direction? What did you expect to happen when you asked students to change their partners? Why did you want students to partner and not form a four-person group?*

I was glad to share my thoughts. By exchanging questions and our thinking with each other, we began to establish a solid foundation of trust on which I knew we would build a strong coaching relationship.

Just as I had encouraged her to reflect, our meeting and her questions prompted me to think about my own practice with this teacher. I asked myself what I had learned about myself that would help me in my coaching practice.

Pondering this question reminded me of the importance of understanding how situational coaching is. There is not just one way to approach adults; coaches must always honor the teacher's voice, choice, and expertise and recognize that collaboration is different from cooperation. I remembered that I wasn't in that job to "fix" anyone. Coaching is not a medical model with grand rounds; it is a model and framework to help teachers become reflective practitioners and implement effective instructional practices that yield positive changes in behaviors, practices, thoughts, and skill sets. I remembered that coaching is like an arranged marriage: teachers cannot choose coaches, and vice versa. Coaches and teachers must work together, respect each other's views, listen fully, and share a vision for schoolwide improvement.

Over the course of several weeks, the history teacher and I worked to identify effective instructional practices and then refined those that she felt needed to be strengthened. We engaged in ongoing conversations implementing the BDA cycle. Together, we identified numerous strategies that would help her students become more involved and participatory. She began planning her lessons with the end in mind and focused on appropriate goal setting; engaging instructional practices that promoted interacting with text; partner and group work; and lesson pacing that allowed students to think, talk to each other, make mistakes, and share their learning without fear of failure. Her students learned to collaborate with their peers and feel more confident about asking questions and admitting what they didn't know. Her capacity and student learning ultimately saw great gains.

Summing Up

Reflective practice, the focus of *A* meetings, is critical for continuous improvement and teaching colleagues to work together, sharing their own skills and learning new ones. Guided by questions such as those in Figure 4.1, it encourages the notion of appraising practice, refining that practice, and applying newly learned skills to grow that practice. Thinking about one's own actions creates an atmosphere that invites transparent conversations, differentiated teacher support, job-embedded professional development, and a deliberate and intentional way to talk about practice and how to go from "good to great." These reflections, based on authentic conversations and an evidentiary trail, inform classroom decisions that positively affect student and teacher growth.

The BDA cycle of consultation offers coaches a way of systematically approaching conversations to encourage open dialogue, transparency, reflection, trust, and teamwork. These elements make the ECIC model a powerful way of changing the teaching and learning equation.

Figure 4. 1 Questions for the *A* Phase

AFTER

In the *after* phase, the coach and the teacher debrief after both have time to reflect on the lesson and the proposed goals. Feedback is timely, specific, descriptive, and nonevaluative.

Coach asks himself or herself these questions:	Coach might ask the teacher these questions:
Assess (Express feelings about the lesson.) • What questions will I ask the teacher about how the lesson went? • What will I say if the lesson did not go as expected? • How will I help the teacher understand that he or she needs more structure and more support?	• As you reflect on your lesson, how do you feel it went? • What evidence did you see that shows whether your goals were met? • What would make this lesson more effective? • What would you change about the lesson for next time?
Recall and Relate (Recollect student behaviors observed during the lesson to support those feelings.) • What kinds of questions should I ask the teacher about what he or she saw students doing or saying? • How will I know that the teacher understands student engagement?	• How did students respond to the lesson? • What did you see students do (or hear them say) that made you feel that way? • Were students able to make connections to prior learning? How did you help them do that? • How do you measure if your students achieved the goals you intended? • What got in the way of your students meeting the lesson's goals/objectives? • Were your students engaged? How do you know? • What will you do differently the next time you teach this content?
Compare (Draw a comparison between student behavior performed and student behavior desired.) • How do I reinforce that student performance is part of ongoing formative assessment?	• Did the lesson meet the intended objectives? Why or why not? • How did what you observed compare with what you planned? • To what do you attribute the difference in performance versus intended outcomes? • How do you know the students were engaged?
Draw Conclusions (Assess the attainment of the lesson goals.) • How will I help the teacher become more reflective about his or her practice? • What did I learn about this lesson and this teacher's learning style? • How can I help this teacher move forward on a learning path for implementation of effective instructional practices?	• As you reflect on the goals for this lesson, what stood out for you about student performance? • What part of the lesson did students enjoy the most? How do you know they enjoyed it? • Which part of the lesson was the most effective in engaging students? Why? • Which activities worked best? Why? • Why did some students perform better than others? What held them back? • What got in the way of students reaching the goals you intended? • What would you modify or change in teaching this lesson again?

Figure 4. 1 Questions for the *A* Phase—(*continued*)

Evaluate (Give feedback about the effects of this coaching session and how this session helps the teacher move forward.) • Thinking about coaching, teaching, and learning, what did I learn about myself as a learner and coach? • What are my next steps with this teacher?	• As you think back over our conversation, what has this coaching session done for you? What is it that I did (or didn't do) that was of benefit to you? What assisted you? What could I do differently in future coaching sessions?

Source: From *Cognitive Coaching: Developing Self-Directed Leaders and Learners* (3rd ed.), by Arthur L. Costa and Robert J. Garmston, 2016, Lanham, MD: Rowman & Littlefield, pp. 329–331. Copyright 2016 by Rowman & Littlefield. Adapted with permission.

5

Preparing the School
for Instructional Coaching

[W]e are adamant that if today's teachers ever hope to be fully supported as life-long learners, they must create and embrace opportunities to model... continuous professional growth.

—Barnett Berry, *Teaching 2030*

Designing and implementing an educator-centered instructional coaching practice is not like flipping a switch—one moment you don't have it, the next moment you do. We have learned through experience about what goes into preparing a district or school for an instructional coaching initiative. The keys to any successful implementation of new thinking are characteristic of a strong teaching and learning environment. Instructional coaching is a long-term investment. All too often practitioners think that anything new should improve learning outcomes almost immediately, even within a year or less. As our own research indicates, it takes time for instructional coaching to show results for teachers and students. It is a habit of mind and practice, and it requires changes in thinking that lead to changes in the school culture. Achieving the mindset that supports coaching is a *process,* and it does not happen overnight.

Creating Enabling Conditions in Your School

Teachers, school leaders, superintendents, boards of education, and parents want their schools to be exciting, creative learning environments that provide every student with an excellent education. In our work, we have identified a number of conditions that provide fertile grounds for successful schools and for effective educator-centered instructional coaching. Taken together, they set a standard for quality.

But we begin with a reminder: these are not absolutes. Few, if any, schools will have *all* of these conditions. Certainly, the more that are in place, the more likely the instructional coaches will be effective. Begin with the end in mind for where you want to go but focus on the reality of where you are at the onset.

The enabling conditions described here are expressions of the power of culture in organizations and depict a school environment open to continuous improvement (Hirsh, 2014). They help to set the stage and climate that supports school transformation.

1. *The desire to change.* You have to want to change. This should be no surprise. It is the bottom line. Starting with a desire to change is the most important prerequisite to being able to change. Then come the hard questions: *Why do you want to change? What inspired the desire for change? What kinds of change do you want to see happen? What outcomes are you hoping to achieve?*

The best approach is transparency—a school community coming together to talk about what the current climate is, how the climate could be more conducive for teaching and learning, and what would help it change. The discussions must be nonjudgmental, reflective, and aligned with the schoolwide improvement plan. They must be a collective endeavor that includes the constituents who will be affected.

But remember that change for its own sake is not an answer. Change does not necessarily mean that things will be better. School communities need to carefully and thoughtfully think through the "why" before they can figure out "what" will help them make change happen.

2. *Shared goals and vision.* Do teachers, school leaders, staff, and community share a common set of goals and a clear vision for the future of the school? It helps if all concerned are pulling in the same direction. Where are you and where do you want to be? Be clear and precise. Don't overreach. Be sure there is broad agreement on what you want to do *before* you think about how you will do it. Articulating goals and a vision is essential to figuring out how to get there. Convening focus groups to discuss the needs of the school community, prioritizing the needs, identifying goals around those needs, strategizing ways to achieve those goals, and developing a timeline and an action plan can help construct a shared vision and shared responsibilities for prompting school transformation.

3. *Good communications across staff and between leadership and teachers.* Good communications and teamwork are essential to effective instructional coaching. Poor communications can result in a noncooperative environment: teachers do not talk or share with one another; teachers are suspicious of leadership (and vice versa);

no one admits that they do not have "the answer"; everyone is protective of his or her bit of turf and unwilling to say anything that seems to suggest they "need some help" or would benefit from it. The list goes on. Schools are healthy when teachers and school leaders are not defensive, are willing to listen to one another, learn from one another, and are comfortable with recognizing that they may not individually know all they need to in order to promote quality teaching and learning.

Holding regular meetings for which notes are recorded and publicly posted enables all to see the progress of the plan and invites participation in an open and risk-free environment. Although passion for change is critical, emotional "I" statements may hinder progress. Staff members can disagree without being disagreeable.

4. *Support for collaboration among staff and between school leadership and staff.* This condition is often a significant stumbling block. Instructional coaches rely on sharing knowledge and finding ways to help teachers and school leaders help one another. It is all about transparency. Suspicion, insecurity, or intimidation will get in the way. If instructional coaching is a desirable direction, building a community of trust that is open to collaboration can smooth the pathway. In a sense, this condition is an extension of "good communications," as described above. The difference, however, is that collaboration enables nonevaluative interaction, an important goal for all instructional coaches.

One of the most effective ways to support change is for the school leadership to dedicate time for coaches and teachers to work together in a confidential, risk-free atmosphere. This is "made" time, not "found" time. That means that schedules include dedicated time to work with colleagues, time that is sacred and not dismissed by the administration to use the coach for other, less important tasks.

5. *A school leadership team that can think creatively about how to achieve school improvement.* The old ways are the old ways. Sometimes they are the best ways; sometimes not. School leadership team members have to think outside the box. They cannot and should not rely only on what they know and what they "think" works. Schooling is increasingly complex; the demands on leaders are nearly overwhelming. A recent study (Grissom, Loeb, & Master, 2013) found that principals actually spend little time on matters of curriculum and instruction, which should hardly surprise anyone in education today. Add in increasing rigor in state curriculum standards, more-demanding statewide student assessments, and a host of issues around teacher support and effectiveness, and what we have is a prescription for overload. Under the circumstances, school leadership has to be willing to step back and find ways to gather the collective wisdom of the school staff as a source of ideas and strategies for improving teaching and learning. A creative school leadership team recognizes the talent pool that can be tapped at their school and in their district.

Rigidity and clinging to the way things have always been done might be comfortable, but looking for new approaches can make a big difference for teachers and students. Great leaders are not reckless, but they do not shy away from new ways and are willing to assume some creative risks in the quest for school improvement.

Innovation and collective problem solving are critical for change. The school leadership team needs to partner with staff members and honor their voice and choice, allowing flexibility to try new things without fear of failure. Focus groups that are established at the onset and given the independence to follow through from construction to appraisal of what worked effectively can make a difference in school change. For school transformation to occur, staff members must be part of the thinking, planning, and delivery.

6. *Understanding how adults learn.* It is easy to overlook the very real differences in how adults and children learn, but understanding adult learning is a key to developing effective working relationships with teachers and school leaders and helping them change. There is extensive research in this area (see Figure 1.1 in Chapter 1 for comparisons of adult and child learning styles), and adhering to best practices is essential to implementing strategies that will promote professional learning. So much of coaching is based on one-on-one interaction. A strong foundation in adult-learning theory helps build both trust and support for the work that coaches do, especially in understanding that teachers are valued practitioners even when they work with a coach.

Coaches honor adult learning by involving staff members in developing a relevant professional development plan that is aligned with the school improvement plan. Administrators need to allow coaches to establish the professional development schedules with staff, co-facilitate sessions where appropriate, and encourage coaches to meet one-on-one with staff to ensure that the professional development sessions lead to professional learning.

7. *Receptivity to new ways of thinking about professional development and professional learning.* Professional development is often an afterthought. Frequently, specific days are set aside for state- or district-proscribed activities that are often led by a consultant, a publisher, or a program vendor and not tailored to a school's specific needs. School-designed opportunities are rare. As a result, professional development tends to be disconnected and, at best, only marginally relevant to teachers' instructional priorities. Does it have to be that way? Professional development is not cost free. Between staff time and hard-dollar expenditures, professional development typically consumes 2 to 5 percent of a school's budget (Gulamhussein, 2013). There are, however, many ways to think about how these funds are spent. Instructional coaching represents a different approach to organizing and implementing professional

development. To the extent that school leaders are willing to consider alternatives to the "one-and-done" professional development tradition, a more targeted and personalized approach can be accomplished by instructional coaches who provide follow-up and sustainable implementation of new learning. For this to happen, the school leadership team must be willing to do things differently and examine how best to collaborate on developing a vision for the school, honoring teachers' voices.

By definition, instructional coaches are skilled practitioners who build trusting relationships with their teaching colleagues. Administrators need to capitalize on the coaches' strengths and respect from the staff so that coaches and teachers can organize a grassroots approach to discovery, working together to plan the kind of professional development that becomes ongoing, sustainable professional learning.

8. *Making the best use of time for professional development and professional learning based on an instructional coaching model.* Time is in short supply, but planning professional development based on an instructional coaching model will take time—time to design how it will work in the school, to put teams together to identify needs, and to help teachers determine their individual needs and wants. Building a coherent, aligned effort requires a good deal of organization. Teachers and school leaders are already challenged to do what needs to be done to make it through the day. An overlay of new responsibilities may be viewed as one thing too many. In addition, too often a new initiative is proclaimed without proper planning and preparation. As a result, the reaction is "This, too, shall pass." That said, it is a matter of priorities. A carefully articulated professional development plan, co-designed by staff members and implemented with an instructional coach, can yield big dividends in terms of professional and student learning.

Effective use of coaching time is intentional and deliberate. Focus group meetings must include attention to addressing the needs as proposed by the staff, allowing them to collaborate on ways to support those needs, and reflecting on how those needs were met.

9. *Patience.* Besides time, patience is another thing in short supply in the world of K–12 education. If a new initiative (whatever it is) does not show results in a year, it often disappears. But deep down, policymakers and practitioners alike know that schools and schooling are so complex that evidence of effectiveness does not come overnight. If the objective is to find a silver bullet, instructional coaching will not provide one.

Instructional coaching unfolds over time as coaches and teachers build trust, focus on achieving the mission, and recognize that teachers and school leaders must learn how to learn—from one another as well as from coaches. No one is an expert, but together, everyone becomes a member in a community of learning and practice, sharing a vision about how to build teacher capacity and improve student learning. The payoffs in classrooms can be significant. To be effective, coaching requires a deliberate plan for elaborating how coaches will support the vision of schoolwide improvement. Patient policymakers, school leaders, teachers, and parents are willing to wait a reasonable amount of time for evidence of improved outcomes. Expecting immediate results will undermine the effort, and so patience is required when discussing expectations. Some things—adding common planning time on teachers' schedules, creating a shared vision for change, establishing focus groups, and generating a needs assessment—can change almost immediately. Congratulations and pats on the back are in order for these small but crucial steps. However, changes in outcomes take longer. Planning, revisiting, refocusing on the needs, debriefing, re-evaluating the successes—all of these take time, and administrators are wise to periodically remind the staff that schoolwide improvement will not occur overnight.

10. *Understanding how issues of confidentiality fit into the equation.* Respect for confidentiality is one of the basic elements for helping instructional coaches succeed. It is how coaches gain the trust of teachers and school leaders. Coaches must be able to navigate between those wanting help and those demanding better performance. Many school leaders recognize that improving practice is a balancing act—teachers have to be amenable to change, have ideas about what they want to change, be comfortable asking for assistance, and not feel as though they are being "evaluated" (for better or worse) while they are given support. Confidentiality is a cornerstone to effective instructional coaching. If the environment is safe and supportive, teachers are more willing to take risks to improve their instructional practice. They will be ready to make mistakes without fear of failing. That's how they will learn what works in their classrooms.

Coaches should be selected not only for their content knowledge but also for their ability to establish solid, trusting relationships with staff members. Ideally, coaches have demonstrated effective interpersonal skills that show respect for confidential, collegial interactions. Administrators need to understand that confidentiality is critical for implementation and not breach that confidentiality by asking coaches about their interactions with teachers. Administrators need to make themselves visible and see what is happening in classrooms that is having a positive impact on student learning, rather than ask the coach for updates.

These 10 conditions are important for building a successful instructional coaching initiative. Certainly, it is highly unlikely that all of them will be present at the same time in a school. Each one, however, can be achieved. Our experience is that schools intentionally build toward securing as many of them as they possibly can, knowing that despite the inevitable bumps in the road, lasting, meaningful learning will take place.

Getting Buy-In by Making the Case for Instructional Coaching

Whose support is critical? The list is not surprising: superintendents, principals and school leaders, boards of education, teachers, and parents. In any given school community, one of these players may be more important than another, but each will have a role to play. Each needs to be consulted or at least apprised of the logic underlying the reasons for promoting instructional coaching in their school. Make no mistake, bringing a coaching initiative to a school requires political acumen. Initiators need to provide information describing what instructional coaching is, how it works, and how it has been done elsewhere; data to support the choice of instructional coaching as an appropriate schoolwide improvement strategy; and evidence that instructional coaching will lead to positive outcomes as compared with other strategies or ventures also competing for scarce resources (time and money). Ultimately, a clear justification is essential.

Gaining support for instructional coaching requires preparation and dialogue. Everyone affected by coaching should be included to the extent that they can or want to be involved. Those promoting instructional coaching must be prepared to answer questions such as the following.

- *How will instructional coaching improve student outcomes?* For this question, get ready to discuss how research (as cited earlier in this book) shows that instructional coaching leads teachers to make positive changes in their instructional practice, leading to an increase in student engagement and learning (see also the Key Findings from the Pennsylvania Institute for Instructional Coaching (PIIC) Teacher and Coach Survey Report at http://piic.pacoaching.org/images/PIICdocuments/Research_and_Eval/piic%20summary%20report%202015_01-13-16%20pdf.pdf).

- *Why instructional coaching rather than something else?* When faced with this question, point out that schools need to assess the effectiveness of the professional development they offer. "Drop-in" professional development is not effective; nor is the effort of an outsider who doesn't know the school culture but tries to tell the staff what they need. Having a skilled practitioner do ongoing work, side-by-side with teachers, promotes the notion that learning takes place all day, every day.

- *What evidence is there that schools with instructional coaching improve their outcomes?* Share research from www.pacoaching.org for data, and the research cited at the beginning of this book.

- *Will every teacher have to participate?* Convince doubters that instructional coaching is not a deficit model and works most effectively when coaches can "work with the willing," with many teachers participating. That is not always the case, however, especially if the principal dictates the teachers with whom the coach will work. When that happens, it behooves the coach to expand the coaching cohort of teachers to include other staff members who want to work with the coach. Remember, coaching is not a deficit model; it doesn't work effectively if teachers feel they are required to work with the coach because there is something "wrong" and they must be "fixed."

- *How will coaches be chosen? What skills do they need that will make them qualified for the job?* To answer this question, point out that most school districts create a job description that includes the skills and competencies that are necessary for implementing an effective instructional coaching model. In a nutshell, advocate for putting on paper that coaching candidates should demonstrate their understanding of the following: subject-area content and literacy-based strategies, basic tenets of instructional coaching, principles of adult learning, effective instructional practices, data collection and analysis, assessment strategies, and theory of change.

- *What does a coach's schedule look like?* Stakeholders need to understand that coaches ideally need daily release time to work with their teaching colleagues. Some schools have full-time coaches; others have part-time coaches. The amount of daily time devoted to instructional coaching helps determine the expectations. Each day's activities, however, need to include working with staff members implementing some phase in the BDA cycle of consultation.

- *How will we know if it is "working"?* Stakeholders will start to notice a change in culture in which professional conversations become the norm in the building and staff members collaborate and generate professional development sessions that meet the needs of their students. Those professional development sessions create ongoing professional learning opportunities where teachers collaborate and plan, discuss, debrief, and revise their thinking so that their students' needs are continuously addressed.

These questions are not easy to answer, and in other chapters we address some in more depth. The point, however, is that coaching cannot be forced on a school community. Sometimes exasperated, overworked, and worried school leaders institute coaching because they think coaches will "fix everything." This is not the right reason to hire coaches. As noted earlier, a healthy school community adopts instructional coaching because it has confidence in the ability of teachers and school leaders to improve instruction through collaboration.

The Cost of Coaching

It is impossible to ignore the fact that much of what is done, or not done, in schools depends on money, which is the case for every school program that is not part of the required curriculum. Budgets are tight. Funds directed at anything but meeting basic needs are scarce. That said, we recommend that the issue of cost be addressed head on, understanding that instructional coaches should not be an "add-on" but rather an integrated part of the faculty. Coaching is not an intervention; it is an approach that offers nonevaluative, one-on-one support to teachers by a skilled, experienced practitioner.

Across the many districts and schools where we have worked, a few strategies and approaches have helped mobilize support for instructional coaching. Although coaching can be a cost-effective solution to improving instructional practice and increasing student engagement and achievement, the case must be made.

How Much Will an Instructional Coach Cost?

The cost of an instructional coach will vary, of course, from school to school, district to district, and state to state. Typically a full-time instructional coach costs about as much as a teacher with the same number of years of service. Coaches rarely are given their own line item in a budget. They are teachers, so that is the line item, just as a coordinator of a specific program is not an added cost, per se, but a teacher who has another role in the school.

There are three typical approaches to funding: (1) a coach is hired as a teacher and is part of the school allocation; if the coach initially starts as a part-time coach and part-time teacher, the goal is to morph that part-time coaching role into a full-time role the following year; (2) a coach may be supported by reallocating funds for traditional professional development, and that money is set aside for the coach's salary and benefits; or (3) the coach may be hired with "soft money" through external funding that pays for the coach's salary and benefits. Although the first two options are the ideal, the third can be an alternative, especially if the school leadership begins planning from the beginning that the soft-money stream will become part of the operating expenses the following year. The critical point is that those making decisions must think about the resources they have and how they will allocate those resources and sustain the funding to make the greatest long-term impact on student learning.

We have seen instances where a school thought the position of coach was so important that there was the collective will (among school leader, teachers, parents, school board, and superintendent) to "trade" a teacher for a coach. This took an extraordinary effort, supported by well-documented gains in student outcomes and true community collaboration. Later, after seeing the coach's positive impact, the school leader was able to persuade all concerned that spending hard-dollar revenue in this way was well worth it. Additionally, the school leader was able to reallocate some professional development funds for coaching, recognizing that the instructional coach, indeed, was the leader of the school's professional development program.

In some cases, schools have funding set aside to "purchase" consultants to provide drop-in professional development for the staff. These are cases in which information is shared but rarely followed by ongoing support to discuss implementation. This approach is an expensive proposition—schools pay for professional development but then must wait for the consultant to come back and answer questions about a practice that may have occurred some time ago. It is not real-time or side-by-side support; this kind of professional development is done *to* teachers, not *with* teachers. When compared to the cost of a full-time coach who is on staff and can be reached all day, every day to provide ongoing support to teachers, funding for the drop-in consultant does not appear to be an efficient use of limited resources.

Risks and Rewards of Soft Money

Many schools and districts are in states that provide funding for coaches from a variety of federal and state grants for innovation or school improvement. There is danger, however, in such dependency. The good news is that these kinds of funds are commonly available. The bad news is that funds from these sources are like a drug—a habit hard to break and especially painful when or if the funds disappear or diminish (as so often happens with soft money). Many of the school leaders with whom we have worked have initially used soft money for coaches, but they begin to think about sustainability right from the beginning, putting a plan in place for expeditiously transitioning to hard money. This means working to make certain that the instructional coach provides valued assistance to teachers, monitoring metrics to document effectiveness, and continually making the case for the coach as central to the school's mission. These are the kinds of leaders who hold the coaching responsibilities sacred and protect the role designed accordingly. (See Figure 5.1 for a table describing some soft-money sources that are often used to fund coaches.)

Figure 5.1 Soft-Money Sources for Funding Coaches

Federal Title Funds	Funds available under the Elementary and Secondary Education Act (ESSA) of 1965, as amended (*Every Student Succeeds Act*), can be directed toward instructional coaching. The following titles could be used to help fund and support instructional coaching: • Title I—Improving Basic Programs Operated by the State and Local Education Agencies • Title II—Preparing, Training, and Retaining Teachers, Principals, and Other School Leaders • Title IV—21st Century Schools • Title V—State Innovation and Local Flexibility (Rural Education)
Rural Education Achievement Program (REAP)	Under ESSA, rural education is funded under Title V. These funds target small rural districts and can be combined with other federal, state, and local funds to support instructional coaches.
Program Improvement Funds	There may be additional funding available through ESSA for schools and districts identified for improvement that may support instructional coaching.
Transferability	Larger urban districts may be eligible under ESSA to combine some of the federal funding under several Titles to support instructional coaches.
General Funds	If the school staff believes that coaching will make a difference, budgets related to the district's general fund can be adjusted to accommodate a coaching initiative.
Pooled Resources	It is common for districts to cooperate and share services. Federal regulations allow school districts to pool resources to share services among several schools. One district agrees to be the fiscal agent, and the funds flow through that district to pay for the shared activities. Districts can pool funds to hire an instructional coach.

All too often, schools and districts do not go through a planning process to segue from soft to hard money. When the soft-money source dries up, there is no way to sustain the instructional coach, no matter how effective that coach has been. Some schools and districts have designed compromises to address the funding issue: sharing a coach between or among sites (which diminishes the benefit of onsite support every day), supporting only a part-time coach (although recognizing that a part-time coach is not likely to have the same impact as a full-time one), or training an existing staff member (e.g., a librarian) to fulfill some of the duties of a coach. Needless to say, these kinds of compromises take a toll on the coach's capacity to meet the needs. No matter how well conceived, it is hard for us to recommend such weak "second-best" strategies.

The bottom line is this: educator-centered instructional coaching is not cost free. Although the optimum solution is to use the school's operating funds to ensure that coaching is an integral part of the school's improvement plan, initially that might not be the case. To work well, ECIC requires a commitment from the entire school community and a powerful strategy to ensure funding that will support coaching beyond the short run.

Summing Up

Consider the qualities that make for the success of an instructional coaching initiative. Think about each in the context of the school environment. From the start, consider which qualities are most important and make sure that they are understood and in evidence. Bring in an instructional coach for the right reasons, and carefully manage funding sources. Don't look for a "quick fix" (that can only disappoint), and make certain that the coach has the supports essential to fostering change in teaching and learning.

6

Setting the Stage for the Work Ahead

Whether coaches will make an impact on teaching and learning depends, at least in part, on the district's ability to identify the right people for the work.

—Joellen Killion and Cindy Harrison, *Taking the Lead*

A strong beginning makes all the difference. The hiring process is an opportunity to articulate needs, define expectations, and ensure that the instructional coach, once selected, is a good fit for a particular school. We describe here a rather precise selection process, intended to give the school leader and staff, as well as the coach, a chance to set the ideal stage for the work ahead.

This chapter discusses nuts-and-bolts issues—identifying needs and defining the role of the coach; designing a job description for the coach; circumstances that affect start-up; and designing a scope of work.

Identifying Needs and Defining the Role

Selecting a coach begins with a basic assessment of needs that is focused on two things:

- Identifying staff's professional development interests and needs, which is important because the coach should be a leader in the design and execution of the school's professional development plan while working to build teacher capacity
- Explicitly describing the skills and capabilities required in the coach job description that align with staff's professional development needs

Making a good hiring decision requires clarity about how a coach will be expected to contribute to helping the school achieve its goals for schoolwide improvement. This is *not* a perfunctory exercise. It is a deep assessment with purpose and focus. Everyone who has a stake in the coach's success—school leaders and teachers—should have some voice in the process. All too often coaching job descriptions read more like wish lists than reliable descriptors of a role, or they are too general to be useful for identifying the kind of coach needed or for helping the coach understand the role. Make the needs assessment count. Always remember that good coaching is about adults working with other adults to improve instruction. The following sections present examples of the kinds of questions that might be asked.

Why Do We Need a Coach and What Are the Most Important Things We Want the Coach to Do?

Coaching requires resources, so it is important to understand exactly why the school wants to have a coach. Why coaching instead of some other investment? Which school goals will the coach help achieve? Articulating goals and objectives is a useful outcome of the needs assessment, as it helps define the skills the coach should have. Under any circumstance, the needs assessment can be used to define the scope of work and to give the school leader and a newly selected coach insight into the parameters of the role. It is an opportunity to distinguish what the coach *will* do from what the coach *might* do. It also sets some boundaries, effectively saying what the coach will *not* do. One principal we worked with spoke of how clear expectations made all the difference.

My school needed to begin with the clear expectations of what the coaching role entails. We needed to recognize that coaches are not evaluators, supervisors, "the expert" content specialists, or the "fixers." My coaches support their teaching colleagues by helping them implement effective instructional practices, not evaluating whether or not teachers are effective. That's left to me as a principal to observe and evaluate. Our coach visits and strengthens practice; she respects the confidential nature of [coaches'] relationships with teachers so they are not "whistle blowers" who report to the building supervisors. Rather, they encourage the administrative team to learn alongside of the teachers and walk around the building to see how the professional development plan has been actualized. Above all, the instructional coaches in my building are not substitute teachers providing regular coverage so teachers can do other things.

In contrast to this situation, a coach we worked with had no clear expectations when he became a coach. Without the benefit of a shared vision with the principal, the expectations were unclear and his effectiveness in working with his teaching colleagues compromised, as the following illustrates.

The Outcome of Unclear Expectations

Mr. Winters had been a coordinator for a PLC in his school for four years. At the start of the new school year, the principal asked him if he would like to become the school's instructional coach. The school community wanted to adopt a reform model and hoped that coaching was the answer. Mr. Winters accepted the position but, unfortunately, he did not have any time to prepare for his new role, nor did he know enough about instructional coaching to design an action plan about how he was going to approach his new role.

One month later, the coach was still unsure about his role. He continued to meet teachers in the faculty lounge, the teachers' cafeteria, the hallway, and the parking lot, not really sure what to offer them. Of course, they didn't know what to expect either. This was a clear case of not knowing what the schoolwide vision was for improvement or how instructional coaching could help accomplish that goal.

Two months later, the coach was focused on being an implementation coach; that is, helping only the teachers who asked how to implement a piece of the science curriculum, as that was his area of certification. He did not get around to the other subject area teachers and devoted most of his time to discipline, student attendance, and cultural events, the requirements for his previous coordinator position.

At the end of the year, the principal met with the coach and expressed his dismay at not seeing a complete transformation of instructional practices while conducting his administrative observations. The coach reminded the principal that they never met to discuss expectations or to inform the staff about the role of the instructional coach and how that differed from his role as coordinator. The staff had no idea what to expect and the coach had no idea what to offer. This was a clear case of misunderstanding and miscommunication, as the school community developed a flawed idea of what and how instructional coaching functions.

With Whom Will the Coach Work?

Will the coach support teachers across all content areas? Will the coach do just program implementation (e.g., support a new reading program), or work with teachers at only one grade level, or something else? As we have made clear throughout this book, we prefer that instructional coaches not be confined to working strictly with teachers of only one "type"—for example, just math teachers, or teachers from one grade level, or teachers who are performing poorly, or new teachers. If instructional coaches are thus limited, the potential power of their practice is diminished and tends to be seen as a "fix-it" model. The coach is inhibited from successfully accomplishing a primary objective of the role: promoting professional development and professional learning for *all* teachers and helping each practitioner go from good to great. Because everyone can benefit from working with an instructional coach and because a good instructional coach wants to engage all teachers, consider carefully how the coach's clientele is defined. We promote a very broad conceptualization of the coaching goal: *the instructional coach is a key leader in professional development who seeks to improve the quality of instruction across the curriculum.* Coaching only a select group of teachers suggests a deficit model, the antithesis of what educator-centered instructional coaching is designed to do. Remember, coaches offer differentiated, ongoing, job-embedded professional development in a safe environment, focusing on schoolwide improvement, building teacher capacity, and increasing student engagement through real-time support. They offer specific feedback designed to improve practice. This is a collective endeavor; everyone wants to improve their craft.

Looking Back on Ellen's First Coaching Job

In my first coaching role, I became a coach in the school where I had taught. I thought it would be easy to change my role, but I soon learned otherwise. The principal directed me to work with some teachers, my former teaching colleagues, whom the principal determined needed extra support; that is, the administrators identified teachers who had a "learning plan" that included working with a coach to prevent an "unsatisfactory" rating.

I didn't realize at the time that not everyone taught the way I did; I just expected all of the teachers to be willing participants who wanted help. I didn't realize that as soon as I was "assigned" to work with these teachers, the coaching line of confidentiality had been crossed. Without any formal training in the art of coaching, the principal and I discussed the teachers' strengths and weaknesses, thereby breaching all confidentiality. If the principal told a teacher to approach me, then the perception of coaching and the outcomes would have been different. As soon as I approached the teacher and said that the principal asked me to work with him or her, that was evaluative and crossed the bounds of privacy. Because the school knew that the principal asked me to work with what he termed "marginal" teachers, the staff refused to participate because they were afraid that they, too, were considered needy. This deficit models eliminated the chance of honest and valuable reflections needed to improve practice at first.

It took a long time for me to turn the situation around and help colleagues understand that coaching is a collaborative effort to improve outcomes and that working only with teachers who needed support was counterproductive; that even those who are skilled practitioners (think performing arts) could benefit from a coach to help refine their practice and skill set, and that going forward, confidentiality would be a priority.

How Will the Coach's Effectiveness be Assessed?

It is worth considering from the outset how the school leader and teachers can come to understand whether the coach is accomplishing what he or she is asked to do. This is not so much about formal evaluations of performance as it is about establishing a clear understanding of what constitutes effective coaching. As we will discuss in other chapters, because instructional coaches do not work directly with students and because they work confidentially with teachers, understanding a coach's effectiveness requires some tailored strategies.

An assessment can be simple or complex, formal or informal, but should be *specific* to coaching and the coach's role. It can be developed by input from focus groups, surveys, interviews, or other means. The important point is that the process should include all the parties likely to have contact with the coach. Remember, this is an assessment of the coaching model as dictated by the job description and explicit roles for coaches, and it helps to ensure understanding of the model and the level of support the coach, once hired, will receive.

The Job Description

Once the needs assessment is complete, the next step is writing a job description. The document we use to help schools develop their job descriptions includes the following kinds of information:

- A preamble describing the school's mission, along with school, student, and staff demographics
- A specific enumeration of roles and responsibilities
- A description of qualifications

Most districts' job descriptions for instructional coaches include basic qualifications, preferred qualifications, general responsibilities, and specific functions of the job. (For an example, see the Pennsylvania Department of Education job description for coaches in Appendix A.) Statements such as the usual "Perform duties as assigned by the principal and director of curriculum and instruction" will be specific to a district's improvement plan. Key points to consider include the coach's skills in creating positive relationships with staff; demonstrating knowledge of evidence-based literacy practices; understanding data analysis to assess student needs; facilitating ongoing, relevant professional development that leads to professional learning; and providing differentiated support to teachers across all content areas.

Candidates for coaching positions should be interviewed by school leaders, teachers, and other school staff with whom the coach is likely to interact. Optimally, the coach begins work with support from the entire school community, recognized as a professional who will help all teachers improve their instructional skills.

Coaches are selected in many different ways, but ultimately they must be a good fit for the school or district. Because "all hiring is local," we are not in a position to generalize what makes one candidate better than any other. That said, our experience suggests certain characteristics and behaviors of effective coaches, including the following:

- Is a good listener, a good communicator, and articulate
- Respects differences among those being coached
- Knows how to build relationships
- Understands the importance of asking questions and is skilled at the art of questioning
- Provides guidance and support in the implementation of an evidence-based, comprehensive literacy learning plan across all content areas
- Is collaborative and cooperative
- Understands adult learning theory and knows how to apply it in the work of coaching
- Practices reflection and helps teachers reflect
- Has deep content knowledge in a particular content area
- Can model effective practice

- Can skillfully gather, analyze, and share data, and knows how to identify effective research-based practices
- Capable of presenting and facilitating professional development

Clearly, it is difficult to find all of these qualities in a single candidate, but the hiring process is an opportunity to see who has a good complement of them.

One other point worth mentioning: both school leadership and the coach benefit if hiring takes place well before the coach begins working with teachers. Coaches have a lot of preparatory work to do. For example, a newly appointed coach needs to be a self-starter and self-learner. Reading extensively about adult learning and coaching provides a starting point from which the coach can generate the first to-do list. Other prep work includes gathering demographic information, obtaining the school's PD calendar to identify scheduled events and determine which topics are teacher driven; reviewing the school's improvement plan and identifying some topics for future PD sessions; planning mini professional development sessions where a short topic of interest can be shared, followed by appointments for one-on-one conversations; and reviewing teachers' schedules to determine common planning time among and between departments or grades.

A longer lead time enables coaches to be introduced appropriately as the instructional coach (even if the coach is already a staff member) and get a head start at understanding the complex coaching role. Sometimes coaches are hired at the last minute (such as when a funding source emerges), but often the decision to hire occurs well ahead of the school year. The timing of a new hire can make a big difference. The more time a coach has before interacting with staff, the more likely the early coaching experience will have positive results.

Circumstances That Affect Start-Up

The circumstances that bring coaching to a school matter a great deal and affect early opportunities in a number of ways. Here we describe five different entry scenarios, the differences among them, and their effect on the start-up process.

A New Coach at a School That Has Never Had a Coach

So here you are. You have been selected to be a coach at a school that has never had a coach before. Congratulations and, well, yikes! If you have never been a coach, that creates its own immediate challenges. If you are going to coach in an entirely new setting (where you have no "roots") and in a school that has never had a coach (and thus no coaching tradition), you face multiple additional challenges.

You may not know the school leader or many on staff. Further, if you have never coached before, you may not be familiar with or practiced what coaches do or how they do it. Finally, your school staff may have no idea what instructional coaches do and thus not much of a notion of how or when to approach you or how to collaborate with you. And in some circumstances, perhaps everyone from the school leader on down has a strong opinion as to what the coach *should* do. Welcome to the coaching start-up experience. The good news is that you will be able to use what you are reading here to craft your approach to instructional coaching. Starting with a blank slate can be a very positive experience as every staff member learns together.

A New Coach at a School That Has a Coaching History

A variant on the first scenario is the new coach who goes to work at a school that has had coaching in the past. If you are starting your first job as an instructional coach, you will not only need to learn what it means to be an instructional coach and how to do that work; you may also need to help the school leader and staff rethink the coach's role to align with your strengths, which may be similar to or different from those of your predecessors. The challenge is that you must honor and build on the school's past positive experiences but, at the same time, may need to undo preconceived notions of what instructional coaching should look like, as illustrated in the following account.

Ellen Looks Back

Starting a new job is anxiety producing no matter what the circumstances; replacing a person who previously held that position is doubly nerve-wracking! When I started coaching, I was assigned to a school that had implemented a coaching model for the previous two years. By their own admission, the first year was spent trying to define the concept of instructional coaching for the coach and leadership team, and the second year was spent trying to convince staff members that the coach was needed. From their experience, a coach worked only with those who needed help, not to help colleagues go from good to great. Because the school already had some idea about instructional coaching, I wanted to ensure that I could build on the strengths of their model and figure out ways to embrace what worked and repair those beliefs that were not as successful by their standards. It was really important for me not to ignore what went before and, at the same time, help them understand what effective instructional coaching looks like.

I started by walking around the building and interviewing some staff members. Most were quite willing to tell me everything they knew about instructional coaching and give me advice about how coaching should work. These conversations were very helpful because I was able to generate a needs assessment from their comments and then elicit some volunteers for a focus group to help highlight what had worked in the past and what ideas should be incorporated in a plan for the future. From there, we worked to identify target areas, goals, roles and responsibilities, and action items to achieve the data included in their school plan.

A Veteran Coach at a School That Has *Never* Had a Coach

Many trained instructional coaches accept jobs at schools new to coaching. Although this might seem like an opportunity to use existing coaching skills to quickly mobilize the school to benefit from the coach's experience, often the opposite occurs. What the coach thinks should happen—based on experience—and what the school leader and staff think they want from a coach may be very different. The coach may be asked to do things that are not analogous with her training and experience, making what first appears to be a good opportunity into something far more difficult. Again, the coach must help build awareness of what an effective instructional coaching model looks like and be transparent and collaborative about designing one that meets the school's needs, always focusing on how to achieve the school's goals for continuous schoolwide improvement.

A Veteran Coach at a School That Has a Coaching History

Well, this coach might be lucky, or maybe not. If the coach's approach is consonant with the school's history and the school leader's and staff's expectations, the transition may go smoothly. If the coach has a particular viewpoint that is different from the coaching experience of the school, the transition may not be so easy. This circumstance requires that the coach, principal, leadership team, and teachers collaborate about expectations and review what has worked in the past and what changes might be needed to meet their goals. Remember, coaching is contextual. What worked in a previous situation may not work as well in another coaching environment. Again, all voices must be heard so that the coaching model meets the needs of the school community.

A Part-Time Coach

As schools face ever-increasing fiscal constraints, part-time coaching is an emerging and growing practice, with a profound effect on what the coach can do, and how, while striving to meet expectations. We will address this important issue later, but for now we mention it as another scenario related to the challenge of a successful start-up. An effective coach understands the BDA process and how to tailor the support, while recognizing that full-time support cannot be accomplished with a part-time schedule.

There is one other point to consider. Many coaches become a "new instructional coach" in the school where they currently work. They likely will hear something like this: "Last year you were my peer and colleague. Now you are the coach? I know everything you know. What should I ever expect to learn from you?" This attitude is not uncommon. It just raises another set of issues regarding how a new coach proceeds. We address this challenge in Chapter 8 as we help coaches renegotiate their roles and support their teaching colleagues.

Whether a new or a veteran coach, whether at a school that has had a coach or not, coaching initially is all about building relationships and starting conversations. That said, coaches need to be sensitive to their setting. Designing a strategy to move from introduction to engagement is no small task. Take advantage of circumstance. If they are new to coaching or new to the school, coaches should not expect teachers and staff to immediately seek their counsel. If they are veterans or at a school with a coaching history, coaches should probe what has been done and how teachers have been coached in the past. It all takes time. Hiring a coach is one thing. Actualizing a coaching initiative is quite another, and breaking down real or imagined barriers takes patience, a little nagging, and a great deal of nurturing.

Designing a Scope of Work— An Agreement Between Principal and Coach

Coaches work closely with their principals, and it is important that the relationship gets off on the right foot. In practical terms, that means co-constructing an agreement that clearly spells out the coach's responsibilities. Together, coach and principal share their vision for instructional coaching and decide the specifics of how coaching will influence student learning, instructional practices, and ongoing professional learning for all staff. Although every agreement is different and circumstances vary, certain core elements of the scope of work are universal. These include, but are not limited to, articulating the coach's focus; how the coach will communicate to the principal about what he or she is doing and how it is being done; and how the leadership team will support the coach's work.

Roles and Responsibilities

As we have stated throughout this book, the coach's role is helping to build teacher capacity for and understanding of high-quality instructional practices; this is effectively accomplished through one-on-one, small-group, and whole-faculty professional development. In addition, instructional coaching is nonevaluative and confidential, an exchange between the coach and the teacher as well as between the principal and the coach. All parties involved need to understand the elements of confidentiality as they apply to the instructional coaching process. Other relevant points include the following:

- An instructional coaching model works best when the principal and the coach jointly introduce the concept of instructional coaching and the roles of the coach as soon as the coaching model is adopted.
- The agreement between coach and principal may be very specific. For example, it may state that a portion of the coach's time involves providing ongoing support to teachers, helping them implement effective instructional practices. This includes co-teaching, modeling, collecting data, and visiting classrooms to support specific instructional practices that are mutually agreed upon by the teacher and the coach.
- The agreement between coach and principal might also state, for example, that a portion of a coach's time will be devoted to planning and facilitating small-group and whole-faculty professional development, including mini professional development sessions (weekly) and a more broad-based menu of professional development sessions for the faculty emerging from a staff needs assessment or the schoolwide improvement plan.

Four Challenges to Address in Defining the Coach's Scope of Work

Principals and coaches should work as a team to inspire teachers and to design a professional learning plan that addresses the school's mission and improves instruction and student outcomes. Principals and coaches are allies, not adversaries, and, as noted in earlier chapters, they should commit to building a school culture that honors and supports collaboration and reflection. That said, educator-centered instructional coaching is a disruptive practice; it disrupts the status quo by focusing a spotlight on routine practice with metacognitive questioning about one's teaching. As a result, a variety of issues may emerge that make it difficult to build a positive and collaborative relationship. As the coach and principal work together to co-construct the partnership agreement, here are examples of issues that might be addressed.

Challenge #1: *The principal wants the coach to say who she works with, what she does, what's "wrong" with each teacher, and what is being done to "correct" the teacher's deficiencies.* As noted, it is critical for the coach and the principal to share a vision for school improvement and the coach's role. This is important especially because the rollout of the school's coaching model must enable the staff to understand the coach's role and how the coach will work with them.

Effective coaches maintain confidentiality and use nonevaluative language with teachers. In this example, this requirement poses a problem for Coach Schwin and Dr. Harvey (the principal).

....

Maintaining Confidentiality

Ms. Wei is an experienced teacher and coach. She knows many "tricks of the trade" that she is ready to share with her colleagues. As a respectful and thoughtful coach, she understands that confidentiality is necessary to build trust and help her colleagues make instructional decisions that benefit students without being placed at risk professionally.

At her weekly meeting with the principal, Coach Wei is asked to reveal which teachers are not reaching out for coaching support, which teachers she thinks need support, and which teachers are not implementing the strategies that Coach Wei has been sharing. In addition, the principal asks Coach Wei to give him a copy of the notes that she collects to document her work with teachers. Coach Wei understands that she is evaluated by the principal and does not want to be insubordinate but also realizes that what is being asked of her clearly undermines her relationships with teachers. She knows that the minute she breaches any confidence, her credibility as an effective practitioner and supportive coach will be compromised.

So the question is, what should Coach Wei do to maintain confidentiality on behalf of the teaching staff and yet be responsive to the principal's requests? Here are some suggestions:

1. Take time in an initial meeting with the principal and leadership team to describe the components of effective instructional coaching and share research about how coaching works. In that meeting, discuss the principal's vision and goals for schoolwide improvement.

Discuss how coaches support teachers and identify what tasks fall into the coach's portfolio (and what tasks do not). Codifying the role may best be accomplished with a partnership agreement or memorandum of understanding between the coach and the school leader, taking into consideration the essential functions for that district or school.

2. Make certain that the principal is comfortable with the coach-principal partnership agreement and understands the critical importance of confidentiality between coach and teachers.

3. Co-plan with the principal how best to describe the coaching model to the staff. The staff needs to see that the coach and principal share a vision for the coaching role and schoolwide improvement. The coach should remind the school leader that visiting classrooms is an effective way to determine how well the coach's professional development work is going. This does not breach confidentiality because the school leader is taking note of the strategies promoted by the coach and used in classrooms. Further, ensuing conversations between the principal and coach can explore professional development the coach has provided in small groups and one-on-one without revealing which teacher received individual support.

Challenge #2: *The principal inadvertently undermines the coach's work with mixed messages.* One would like to believe that a principal who chooses to hire an instructional coach understands the benefits of effective teacher professional development and ongoing classroom instructional support. This is not always the case. Here is another example of misunderstandings that can be addressed in the coaching agreement between coach and principal.

Addressing Misunderstandings

Poplar Elementary started the year with a few new initiatives in addition to instructional coaching. When teachers began to grumble about being over-extended, the principal told the staff not to worry—the instructional coach would help everyone implement the new initiatives, which included a newly adopted math curriculum and English language arts series, a new computerized reading program, and an antibullying program for 3rd graders.

With these reassurances, the principal undermined the coach. She effectively rewrote the coach's job description by making the coach responsible for ensuring that the other new initiatives are well implemented instead of protecting the coach's efforts to make certain that teachers would have an opportunity to nourish their own professional growth or to have input about the needs for schoolwide improvement. What should they do to correct this? They could start with the following actions:

1. Coach and school leader need to take a step back and review their partnership agreement and make sure that the coach's responsibilities are clear to all. This should take place at several points during the year or at least annually.

2. Keep "other task" assignments to a minimum; they are add-ons only in extraordinary circumstances. Coaches need to focus on schoolwide improvement.

3. The coach and teachers can form subcommittees to "take the pulse" of the school and collect information about the issues that seem paramount to school success. These subcommittees can form professional learning communities organized around topics of concern. Meeting schedules should be determined with an action plan and a timeline of what actions are needed and who will be responsible for fulfilling them.

4. The coach and teachers need to discuss the school's initiatives and strategize ways to address them. The coach is a liaison to that process, marshalling the teachers and helping them find their own voice, not necessarily responsible for managing their implementation.

Challenge #3: *The principal thinks the coach is just another pair of hands and asks the coach to do a variety of tasks that may or may not be appropriate to the coaching portfolio.* Sometimes principals just don't get it. By "it," we mean the idea of what coaches do and how they support teachers and their classroom instruction. Often principals who have never been coached or mentored themselves think that coaches are classroom aides or assistants who should deliver books, duplicate materials, grade papers, or provide extra hands in the student cafeteria. Some principals think that coaches wait in their office for teachers to ask them for help and in the meantime can be used for any purpose whatsoever. Although a coach may offer help in some circumstances, this should occur only when absolutely necessary, as illustrated in the following.

Maintaining Priorities

For the first month of the school year, Mr. Martinez made deliberate and intentional plans to schedule classroom visits to discuss how he might work with teachers who were interested in being coached. He kept a calendar of his scheduled work by period and topic for administrators but did not include the teachers' names so that the substance of their work together remained confidential. This worked for a while. Coach Martinez was comfortable letting his colleagues know that he, like them, was a learner and that he was looking to them for help in becoming acquainted with their needs and interests.

Unfortunately, his principal did not understand the essential premise for Coach Martinez's efforts. He believed the coach could always break away from his time with teachers to help meet other school needs. When Coach Martinez discussed his role with the principal, they agreed that helping teachers implement effective instructional practices was the top priority. But the coach felt that this conversation may have been "lip service" because he was interrupted several times each week to cover classes; to tutor students in various pull-out programs; and to coordinate, monitor, and administer tests to students. He knew that such distractions were not in his best interests or those of the teachers he supported. He knew that his work should reflect what he and the principal had stipulated in their partnership agreement. Here is how Coach Martinez and his leadership can help him get back on track:

1. Coach Martinez and the principal need to meet regularly to reinforce their understanding of the coaching role and ensure that their goals for schoolwide improvement move forward.

2. Together at a faculty meeting, Coach Martinez and the principal need to build awareness of the instructional coaching process so that the vision and mission of coaching is shared with the faculty.

3. Coach Martinez could design a needs assessment, drawn from conversations with the faculty about the kinds of professional development teachers think is appropriate for schoolwide improvement. Once the list is developed, Coach Martinez could enlist the support of his colleagues by asking who can co-plan and then co-facilitate professional development sessions with him. Because the list of needs was generated from the staff, it is more likely that staff members would participate in ongoing professional development.

4. The needs assessment should be shared with the principal along with a tentative schedule of professional development sessions for the faculty. Once the principal sees the variety of schoolwide needs, he may be more likely to support the coach's schedule.

5. Coach Martinez needs time to plan and collect research for his work with teachers. Every week should be filled with a variety of sessions with teachers, designed to follow the needs assessment that has generated topics of interest.

6. Coach Martinez needs to create a schedule of support following the BDA cycle of consultation to help the principal understand the time commitment needed to work with the teachers.

The *ideal* plan is for all teachers to engage in the full BDA cycle with each coaching interaction, but that may not always be possible, especially if coaching time is limited. In a less than ideal plan (and one that we do not recommend), most teachers will be involved in a *before* planning session; some will be involved in the *during* classroom visit, when the coach either models, co-teaches, or collects data; and most teachers working with the coach will be involved in the *after*, or debriefing, sessions several times during the year. This approach is complicated because a coach needs to see how the plans are actualized and then reflect with the teacher about what happened. Coaching is differentiated by need, choice, and voice; the coaching interactions are individual. The coach must assess the levels of needs— that is, does the teacher need or want *intensive* support (as might be the case for new teachers), *strategic* support (for specific kinds of challenges, desires, or general "counsel" for implementing a new concept), or *independent* support (as might be the case for experienced teachers who need or want to participate in small-group work and require one-on-one support only occasionally). At a minimum, every teacher needs to meet with the coach *for the full BDA cycle various times during the school year.*

Another consideration is that following the BDA cycle may be determined by the work itself. For instance, one teacher may need to work more frequently with a coach around a particular unit of study and not need as much support later, when the unit changes. If, for example, a teacher wants to integrate some digital tools for collaborative writing and is not familiar with that practice, he may approach the coach and ask for assistance in identifying an appropriate tool or may want the coach to help him use the tool in the classroom. Once the teacher has learned about the kinds of digital tools available for collaboration, there may not be a need for the same kind of support. At another time, however, the teacher might want to explore something he is already familiar with and wants only a brief conversation focusing on a specific question. Either way, the conversation in the *before* phase identifies the goals, the data needed, the date for the debriefing, and the roles that both teacher and coach will assume in the *during* phase, followed by the *after* session to debrief and reflect. Although the optimum scenario encompasses all three phases of the BDA cycle of consultation, coaching is situational and therefore may not always look the same.

Challenge #4: *The principal wants the coach to work only with "problem teachers."* As we have said before, coaching is not a deficit model. If a principal "assigns" a coach to work only with "problem" teachers, those teachers will suffer from the stigma that says, "I need to be fixed." How many teachers will seek support if the school philosophy is not schoolwide improvement but, rather, identifying those who need support because they can't "do it right"?

Teachers want to teach to the best of their ability. They should be able to teach students in ways that best meet the students' learning needs. Teachers who strive to meet that goal appreciate and seek out ongoing, nonevaluative coaching. If teachers think the principal has asked the coach to help those who are "troubled," how likely are they to ask for support? Consider the following example.

Disavowing the Deficit Model

When Mr. Davis began as a coach, he and the principal did not establish an agreement about the focus of his coaching or how support would be provided. Initially, Coach Davis saw this as an opportunity to shape the coaching model and reinforce the notion that coaching was not a deficit model. He believed that every staff member should benefit from the opportunity to talk about practice with a skilled, experienced professional in a nonevaluative way. He did not want to be "boxed in" and expected to work with only a subset of teachers. Coach Davis designed his schedule with a cohort approach, in which he cycled through the process of working with different teachers on a rotating basis. He made his groups visible so they knew which cohort of teachers was working with the coach at a particular time. Because he included all the teachers, issues of selection were minimized.

Unfortunately, the principal did not share Coach Davis's vision. He wanted to see a quick turnaround and have the coach work only with those teachers who were identified as "marginal" or "needy." Coach Davis knew that this was not a productive way to approach schoolwide improvement. Here is how he might address this issue:

1. The coach needs to work with the principal and design a coaching plan for the entire staff. If the principal insists the coach work only with teachers that he designates, the coach can still broaden the mix by planning some small-group professional development for the whole staff and finding other ways to gain support beyond the individuals identified by the principal.

2. Even if the principal insists that the coach work only with designated teachers, the coach should share research about effective instructional practices across the school community and always refer to the goal of schoolwide improvement. Deficit models tend to foster low morale because the entire faculty knows who has been designated by the principal as "needing help." It is a breach of confidentiality when the principal announces, albeit through the coach's assignments, that there is a list of teachers with whom the coach will be working.

3. Coaches should meet regularly with staff to share how instructional coaching can help support schoolwide improvement. They should always be looking for ways to provide support for effective instructional practice that can be useful to all teachers. That is one way to slowly introduce school leaders to the idea of voice and choice that teachers should have in their professional development and work with coaches. Many teachers will take ownership of their own roles in the coaching initiative, but only if they play a role in the planning.

These are examples of the kinds of challenges that often emerge after a coach begins work. Each points to the importance of a carefully co-constructed partnership agreement, which can make all the difference in clarifying the role as the coach looks to get footing in the new role and helping the school community to understand the coaching expectations.

Summing Up

The decision to add an instructional coach to the staff should be done carefully and thoughtfully. Before a person is selected, those who will work with the instructional coach need to collaboratively agree on what needs the coach will address. Job descriptions, the selection process, and the ultimate scope of work should be specific and well-articulated so that the new coach, regardless of the school circumstance, will have a clear understanding of how the role will contribute to supporting the school's mission. In turn, once selected, principal and coach need to agree upon the parameters of the role, so that the coach and the staff will understand how the coach is expected to contribute to achieving the school's student learning goals.

7

Preparing to Coach: Guidance for Coaches

The effectiveness of a coach depends on his or her relationships with colleagues in the school building. As the school prepares to adopt a coaching model, the administration must show support and understand the role of the coach. Part of that understanding highlights the line of confidentiality that cannot be crossed. That's how trusting relationships are established and sustained.

—Diane Hubona, Mentor

Once selected, new coaches have a lot of work to do, including critical first steps. Although some suggest that coaching can be intuitive, in fact, effective coaching is not a natural act. By and large, coaching is a learned set of skills that are related to, but different from, teaching. We have seen many schools hire excellent teachers as coaches, only to have them be rendered ineffective because it was assumed that whatever skills they had developed in the classroom could be used to hit the ground running. On the contrary, every instructional coach needs training to be effective. Not every excellent teacher makes an effective coach, but every effective coach must be an excellent teacher.

Basic Tenets of Educator-Centered Instructional Coaching

No matter the background of the person selected to be a coach, a lot of important new learning needs to take place. We believe every instructional coach needs to be aware of the following 10 points about the work.

1. *Always keep two questions front and center: "What am I doing as a coach to help teachers change and improve their practice?" and "How can I help teachers to improve student engagement and student outcomes?"* Instructional coaches work with teachers

to reinforce that what is learned through theory, demonstration, and practice is successfully applied in classrooms. Their work is intentional and deliberate, providing real-time support and specific feedback designed to improve practice.

2. *Understand the basic principles of adult learning.* As described in Chapter 1, adult learning is fundamental to the practice of instructional coaching. Coaches, probably more accustomed to working with students, now must work with teachers and school leaders. To be effective, they need to recognize what it takes to connect with adult learners. A coach who tries to work with teachers and school leaders in the same way as with elementary or secondary school students is not likely to have much success. Although the principles of adult learning are not hard to understand, mastering the methods of reaching these learners can be challenging. Effective instructional coaches adapt the particular logic of adult learning to their practice and recognize that preconceived beliefs and philosophies may affect their efforts, as when a teacher thinks coaches work only with "needy" teachers and thus avoids seeking advice or support for fear of being perceived as needing help.

3. *Understand what collaboration means and how it works.* Instructional coaches work *with*, not *on*, their colleagues, and they should always encourage collaborative conversations between and among teachers. Building strong, trusting relationships with colleagues is critical for opening up discussions about student work, instructional practices, and student learning. But fostering collaboration requires a concerted effort, because it is not natural for teachers, who spend most of their time sequestered in classrooms. Coaches can help fill the void and move the environment from isolation to collaboration. Here are some tips on how to promote effective collaboration:

- Listen actively, without any preconceived notions or assumptions.
- Share ideas and welcome feedback.
- Promote continuous improvement through ongoing conversations, not just one-time interactions.
- Focus conversations on instructional practice and student work.
- Make time to collaborate.
- Practice and model collaboration.
- Give yourself and the teacher the freedom to explore new ideas.
- Collaborate with a purpose.
- "Broadcast" a shared vision for schoolwide improvement.

There is a fundamental misconception about collaborative teaching—co-teaching—with a colleague in the same classroom. Although it might sound risk free, the co-teaching context can be challenging and flawed unless well planned. Here are some suggestions to guide the process:

- Think aloud. Both the coach and the teacher have to discuss the topics, identify the goals, and determine the materials they will use.
- Decide what students need in order to achieve the identified goals and determine what both of you need in order to support the students' understanding of that content.
- Create the formative and summative assessments before implementation.
- Plan for transitions between activities and how to structure those activities (e.g., small group, partners, whole class, and so on).
- Differentiate the teaching so all students have an opportunity to succeed.
- Above all, be transparent and understand that the teacher is the "teacher of record" and you are the supporter.

4. *Understand what sets educator-centered instructional coaching apart from other kinds of coaching.* An educator-centered instructional coach is not the same as a subject matter coach (such as a math or reading coach) or other kind of coach. Educator-centered instructional coaches need to be schooled in the literature that describes *this* approach, one that focuses on working with adult learners, helping teachers apply evidence-based literacy practices, and using a variety of effective instructional practices across all content areas. There are a lot of materials that new coaches can read that will help them prepare for their initial experiences in the field and build their knowledge base. Resources include EduCoach Chat, the Teaching Channel, Edutopia, and a variety of online blogs and instructional coaching sites. Educator-centered instructional coaching, however, is different and requires the kind of thinking outlined in this book. Coaches can also look for supporting materials on our websites at www.instituteforinstructionalcoaching.org and www.pacoaching.org (Pennsylvania Institute for Instructional Coaching, 2016).

5. *Know how to describe what an instructional coach is (and is not) and what your responsibilities will be.* Think for a minute about a coach getting up in front of the school staff on the first day of school. What should the coach say? How does the coach describe "the work"? To accomplish this, coaches must genuinely understand what they will do. At a recent professional development conference, we asked coaches about their most difficult early challenges, and they unanimously said, "Figuring out what a coach does and describing that to others." Here's how a couple of coaches have described their important work.

....

Coach #1: As a coach, I offer various professional development opportunities with the staff. The teachers and I have developed a system of planning, facilitating, and evaluating our professional development that follows the *before, during,* and *after* process of coaching. We conduct needs assessments throughout the year and take these into consideration when planning what to offer. The teachers and I co-facilitate and create lesson plans for all the sessions offered. These are posted on our school wiki for anyone to access. After each session, we ask for teacher feedback, and based on the feedback, we plan for future PDs. Teachers recognize the degree to which their input is valued in this process, and it makes them more receptive to the coaching opportunities offered. I see fostering and encouraging this process as my instructional coaching role.

    Coach #2: In an effort to support my one-on-one sessions with teachers, I wanted to increase my support to teachers and make sure I was meeting their needs. I knew some wanted to work with me but didn't know how to initiate the conversation. So I added a voluntary aspect to our mandatory professional development sessions by offering study groups during the time allotted for these meetings. The study group topics were based on interest levels, coaching conversations, schoolwide action plan items, and books that the teachers wanted to discuss. Before the meetings, teachers signed up for the study group of their choice. Each group determined the schedule for meetings, the appropriate topics, the pace for conversation, action items where applicable, and next steps. Facilitating these conversations and study groups are where my coaching responsibilities rest!

....

    6. *Meet with the principal and the school leadership team to share and discuss their expectations for coaching and the confidential nature of the work.* Write a comprehensive action plan explicitly defining the coach's role and describe the coach's professional development targets and the types of supports that will be available to teachers and school leaders, as well as stating explicitly what is outside the scope of the role. Coaches and school leaders should not work at cross purposes. As noted in the previous chapter, the job description helps to clarify expectations, but new coaches need to spend enough time with school leaders so that both share a common vision about what is needed to promote schoolwide improvement. Problems can arise if the school leader expects the coach to do things one way and the coach does these

things another way. If the school leader expects the coach to focus on some needs and the coach focuses on other things, a roadblock to effective implementation develops. "Face time" with busy school leaders is always at a premium, but new coaches need to build a strong relationship to ensure mutual support and cooperation. They need to meet regularly to discuss ways to improve teaching and learning but *not* to discuss the individuals involved in the implementation.

7. *Strategize about how you will gain credibility and support from teachers and administrators so that you will become recognized as a leader in delivering schoolwide professional development.* New coaches are not always welcomed with open arms. Getting access to teachers is often the greatest single frustration for new coaches.

Nothing in particular will ensure an open door. No one strategy works for all circumstances. But there does need to be a strategy (see Figure 7.1 for some suggestions). As we note in the next chapter, it helps to carefully research (and take an inventory of) the history of professional development activities in the school. Identifying the needs can help pinpoint what kinds of professional learning teachers want and feel are effective in strengthening their practices. The best way to build support is to begin by arranging small-group professional development opportunities without high expectations regarding how many teachers will take advantage of them initially. That starting point often generates one-on-one work with teachers. New coaches need to work with those who present themselves, knowing that these emissaries of goodwill often pave the way for others to follow.

8. *Collect data.* Gather information about the school—that is, student, schoolwide, and community data; schoolwide improvement plans; information about past professional development programs; PD calendar days, where the coach will be working and can meet with teachers confidentially; and other basic facts. Knowing as much as possible at the start will not only build your confidence but also demonstrate your willingness to learn. Gathering the data honors teachers' accomplishments and enables you to make plans around their schedules. For example, if you know that the science department meets on the first Tuesday of each month, getting on their agenda to build awareness of instructional coaching or offering a professional development session can be an access point.

9. *Plan the rollout.* A good first step is to start thinking about a system for effective communication between the coach and teachers. Find out if there are school requirements about putting messages and flyers in teachers' mailboxes. Placing announcements on bulletin boards or other public places in the school can be an effective way to alert staff to upcoming professional development. A good place is also on "stall walls," the space inside the restroom stalls. As you move around the building collecting tidbits of program information, ask teachers how they would

like you to communicate with them—e-mails, notes in mailboxes, text messages, and so on. Be sure to advertise your e-mail address and welcome all kinds of communication, and don't forget to advertise that meeting schedules are flexible and meetings are held in safe, confidential spaces away from classrooms. Regardless of the mode of communication, the messages about effective instructional coaching must be clear, consistent with the school plan, supported by the administrators, noninvasive, and risk free.

Figure 7.1 Ten Ways to Engage Teachers

1. **Clearly describe your role as coach.** Work to achieve transparency so that everyone understands the role of the coach and the ways in which you will work with teachers.

2. **Fully explain the BDA cycle of consultation** and why it is important.

3. **Give teachers voice.** Ask teachers how and what the coach can do to help them.

4. **Interview or survey teachers** to find out what they want and need in terms of professional development. Recognize teachers' contributions in helping shape the agenda.

5. **Listen.** Teachers want to know that they are heard. Open a dialogue to encourage collective problem solving and collaboration.

6. **Start small.** Find supportive teachers who will help co-plan and co-facilitate professional development events. Even if the event is attended by only a few teachers, it is a start.

7. **Model or co-teach** so that others can see that coaches are willing to share their skill and knowledge. Invite other teachers into the classroom and model instructional practices appropriate to the content.

8. **Provide an opportunity for teachers to plan collegially** and discuss their own learning needs and the needs of their students.

9. **Give teachers time to reflect with the coach,** with a commitment that the conversations will remain confidential and strictly nonevaluative.

10. **Be humble.** Coaches are not experts who know everything; they know something about adult learning and they know that they want their colleagues to work together. They are also practitioners who value and respect their peers.

10. *Collaborate from the beginning.* As soon as possible, start collaborating with teachers to co-construct professional development and professional learning goals. Plan a schedule covering items such as these: How many days a week will the coach support teachers? How many periods a day will the coach work with teachers? When will teachers meet with the coach? Start with low-hanging fruit: plan some initial, small-group sessions to explain, explore, and exchange ideas and effective practices

associated with content that interests teachers as indicated by the needs assessment. As noted earlier, these small-group PD situations typically generate the one-on-one sessions as practice moves forward.

> "Coaches should really want teachers to lead the conversations and should listen deeply, because on the surface, teachers may say one thing but have a lot more underneath that needs to be said." —Heather Moschetta, Mentor

Summing Up

The coaching process is not always automatic. The reality is that most teachers are unaccustomed to collaborating with their colleagues. They need time and guidance to understand the confidential, nonevaluative role of a coach. And, as a coach begins working, it is important to learn and understand different ways of engaging the staff and building awareness that constructive instructional coaching is risk free. Although establishing trusting relationships takes time, laying a strong foundation for the work is key to becoming a successful coach. A clear vision of skill building over time is equally important. Coaches can never know all that they need to know, so they must be eager learners. To guide their first days on the job, coaches will never stray too far from their goals as long as they keep two questions front and center: *What am I doing as a coach to help teachers change and improve their practice? What am I doing as a coach to help teachers improve student engagement and student outcomes?*

8

The Journey Begins:
The New Coach

Coaching is a conversation, a dialogue, whereby the coach and the individual inter-
act in a dynamic exchange to achieve goals, enhance performance and move the
individual forward to greater success.

—Zeus and Skiffington, Inspirational Words of Wisdom

Gee, I'm a coach. Now what?

For coaches new to the role, the first days on the job are probably a bit more daunting, but even if you have experience, the role of a coach always requires some adjustments in thinking and actions. Regardless of your experience, the following questions are probably on your mind. If not, they will be!

- How do I begin? What do I do first?
- How do I establish a clear definition of the coaching role?
- What kind of support, and how much, do I want from my administrator?
- How do I get teacher buy-in to the idea of coaching? How do I gain the trust and confidence of teachers—especially the resistant ones—and attract them to my coaching practice?
- How do I encourage teachers who struggle to try new things without making them feel unskilled?
- How do I measure my success?

Think back to the last time you started a new job. No doubt, the early days were exciting but also filled with anticipation and anxiety. You knew and understood how to act and "how things worked" in your last job, but that is—at best—modestly relevant in your new position. Everything has changed. You need to understand new skills, become a part of a different culture, build new collegial relationships, and learn a different work routine. All this takes time and probably comes with considerable stress. As a new instructional coach, you are not walking in, booting up your computer, writing lesson plans, and working with your own students. Quite the contrary. You are embarking on a new and complicated journey—working with adult learners!

What makes the journey especially challenging is that your colleagues—administrators and teachers—also may not be sure about your role and how it fits the needs of your school even though you may have made efforts to clarify this before stepping into the role. You need to take the lead on defining what you will do and how you will do it—all while embarking on a steep learning curve. In the following account, one of our colleagues shares a couple of hard lessons she learned during her first year of coaching.

···

Lessons Learned

My first days were filled with anxiety, trepidation, and excitement. My new role as an instructional coach was in a building I knew well... I taught there previously and knew several of the staff. I was also coaching teachers to use a prescribed curriculum, so I felt comfortable with the content.

Despite my preparation with the scant information on coaching that was available at the time, the first days were not easy. A few colleagues resented me and made me realize that I needed to renegotiate my role with them. I had to help them understand that I was not better than they; I just possessed a different skill set that I was trying to share. I knew that shifting from isolation to collaboration would be challenging, so I started by going to the early adopters, those who immediately invited me into their rooms—only to leave me with their classes! I had to help them understand the importance of their participation and collaboration. In time, we developed a shared understanding and began collaborating using the BDA cycle.

Rule #1: Make no assumptions. I arrived at school early and began walking around the halls to get a feel of the environment in my new position. Knocking on the door of a former colleague, I announced that I was now the new instructional coach and planned to help everyone change his/her practice! With one hand on her hip, my former colleague said, "... And honey, what do you think you'll teach me?" The door closed, and for one year I met her at the threshold, providing her with resources and other "goodies." She welcomed other teachers I brought to her room to watch her practice but never allowed me to cross that threshold. At the end of the year she calmly asked me, "Well, honey, did you learn your lesson? Don't assume we all need or want your help."

Rule #2: Be transparent and sincere. I was not a medical doctor going on grand rounds. I was not a "fixer." I was, however, a practitioner who wanted to talk about instruction, reflective practice, and learning with my colleagues. I had a responsibility to share my understanding of instructional coaching with my colleagues and help them see how coaches are problem-solvers, collaborators, consultants, and critical thinkers... different modes of operation for a variety of situations.

That first year of coaching was an eye opener. I learned a great deal about my teaching colleagues and even more about myself as a learner and listener. I realized that I didn't have an answer for everything and everyone although I started my coaching role with that very misconception that I had all the answers. I learned that the language of coaching is critical... a coach asks and doesn't tell; a coach encourages and is positive; a coach models collaboration by being collaborative and welcoming suggestions from others. I learned that several of my colleagues were teacher leaders but didn't want to move beyond their classroom doors and that was OK; coaching is not for the faint of heart or nervous nellies!

....

This chapter is a practicum on the start-up challenge and is meant to provide structure for both instructional coaches and school leaders. We look at how the coach can organize for the difficult task of building and meeting the needs of a new constituency. We explore first days on the job, consider ways of garnering support and overcoming resistance, and offer suggestions that will help the coach and administrative team launch a coaching model successfully.

Getting Started

Coaches should be prepared to address a number of tasks early in their tenure (see Figure 8.1). All are essential to easing into the role, as they help the coach gain support and show how coaching can contribute to the school's larger mission. How coaches choreograph these early days can have a significant impact on their prospects for success. For both new coaches and veterans, the rollout is critical to overcoming early obstacles and keeping challenges manageable.

Figure 8.1   A Primer for New Coaches

TASKS	ACTIONS
Fine-tune the definition of your role and duties within the context of the new role.	Read everything you can find online and in professional journals about instructional coaching. Talk to other coaches. After you have done your research, write your own description of the coach's role.
Understand the territory and get to know the school inside and out, building on the preliminary data you collected while preparing for the role.	Gather schoolwide data on students and the community; review the professional development calendar; read the schoolwide improvement plan; gather information about the staff, including years of experience, teachers per department per grade level, and each teacher's contact information.
Meet with the principal to discuss roles and expectations.	Discuss roles and responsibilities; the confidential nature of coaching; how information about the coach and the role will be shared with the faculty; and where and when you will meet with teachers. If possible, meet the principal before the first day of the school year.
Meet the school staff—and be prepared!	It is most beneficial if the coach is identified long before the new school year begins. That way, the coach can take the necessary time to collect the data and prepare for the role. Encourage the principal to share his or her vision for instructional coaching at a whole-school faculty meeting and how it can help with schoolwide improvement. (This kind of joint communication demonstrates collaboration and shared thinking. The staff will see that the principal supports instructional coaching from the start.)
Do a needs assessment to identify professional development interests among the staff and write an action plan.	Begin with a grassroots approach by asking around and identifying some topics from the staff members. Then conduct a more formal survey to gather the data about interests and priorities, making sure that the initial topics are included on this list. Then start writing down how you will address these topics and improve instruction. What are your coaching goals—short, medium, long term—and how will you accomplish them? Show how they are aligned to the schoolwide plan. What is your timeline for achieving each goal, and how will you know that you are being effective? Be sure to include time for reflection in your coaching plan. Reflective practice must be modeled regularly until the practice becomes common and second-nature.
Set your schedule.	Think about the mechanics. How will you get and give contact information to teachers? How often will you facilitate small-group professional development, and how many periods per week will you meet and coach teachers one-on-one? Remember, the three-step BDA cycle brings a strong organizational component to coaching. Design your schedule to meet current circumstances, understanding that it will have to be updated regularly as the circumstances and needs change.
Think about how you will market your message.	Think about how you can make your coaching goals—short, medium, long term—known schoolwide. Explicitly tie your goals to the schoolwide plan. Make your timeline for achieving each goal clear to teachers.

In addition to the tasks shown in the figure (which are covered in more detail in the following sections), here are some other points to keep in mind as the new school year begins:

- Start the year with short-term, midyear, and end-of-year goals.
- Design a plan to work one-on-one and in small groups with your colleagues, including collecting, analyzing, and using data effectively.
- Make sure teachers understand that students need multiple daily experiences with speaking, listening, thinking, reading, and writing as expectations in all classrooms.
- Help teachers understand the importance of reflecting in, on, and about practice.
- Begin and end each day by answering these questions: (1) *What am I doing as a coach to help teachers change and improve their practice?* and (2) *What am I doing as a coach to help teachers improve student engagement and outcomes?*

Defining Your Role Once You're On the Job

As we have reiterated throughout this book, if a coach walks into a school without a clear sense of the role, it will be more difficult to define it later. This is not to say that you won't rethink aspects of the job—and refine or even redefine your practice—but you need to know where you are trying to go *right from the start*. You need to clearly articulate the basic elements of your role. Doing so will help when you meet with the school leader, and it will make a difference when describing your role to teachers. Take the time to write a case statement addressing at least these points:

- What is instructional coaching?
- Who will you coach?
- How will you coach?
- When and where will you meet teachers?
- How will you build awareness of the difference between your role as an instructional coach who helps change practice schoolwide over an extended period of time and a "specialist" who intervenes with an immediate student or a classroom problem?
- How will you address questions of and challenges to confidentiality and evaluation?
- How will coaching help achieve the school's goals and objectives?
- If you are a veteran teacher in the school, how will you renegotiate the role as an instructional coach and teaching colleague?

With a case statement in hand, you begin with an advantage. Your statement may not become your "mandate," but without it as a guide, others may tell you what your work is or should be and perhaps lead you in directions that are not consonant with the role. Many coaches have latitude and flexibility in how they do their work because their case statements promoted what they believe in and what they considered to be essential for their coaching. The following account illustrates the importance of thinking ahead and being able to clearly articulate your role.

Ellen Clarifies Her Role

When I transferred to a new school to become the instructional coach, I was unsure how the school community would respond. This was a new endeavor by the school, and I had expectations, prior experience in the coaching role, and the job description for the position. At our first meeting, the leadership team's collective perspective was shared. They did not refer to the job description and decided that I would be the testing coordinator and administrator for all the required standardized testing as well as the "relief" teacher when students needed a room for make-up exams. When I had time, I would certainly be expected to work with teachers who asked for help. From my past experiences, I knew that this was not the role of an instructional coach. I reiterated the role and function of effective instructional coaching, distributed some articles of interest, and asked questions about the schoolwide improvement plan and how I could help the school community achieve those goals. If I had not thought about or planned my role nor had prior knowledge, the leadership team's misunderstanding of the instructional coaching role would have determined how I worked, thus eliminating the opportunity for me to influence teaching and learning.

As previously noted, coaches sometimes know they will have a position in the spring or summer before the start of the school year. If that is the case, this interim "quiet period" can best be used to explore the role, talk with other coaches, and prepare for the important conversations you will have with the school leader, teachers, and staff.

Getting to Know the Territory

No two schools are alike. No two schools have the same needs. Although the nature of the school and the community in which you are coaching may seem quite clear to you, gather the data anyway. The information—a strategic notebook—will make the context easier to understand and clarify the coaching environment. It reminds the coach of all the factors that influence student performance. Elements of a school profile might include the following:

- *Demographics.* Who attends the school? What is the composition of the student body by grade? What percentage of students are ELL, economically disadvantaged, and so on?
- *Student performance.* How have students performed on standardized tests over the past *three* years—by grade, gender, socioeconomic status, ELL, and other metrics?
- *School mission.* What is the school's mission? How can instructional coaching help support the school's mission?
- *School improvement plan.* The plan can serve as a good way to identify priorities.
- *Inventory of school-based professional development activities* for the past two years. Are there professional learning communities? If so, how often do they meet? How do participants select their PLC? How are topics for PLC meetings determined?
- *Leadership and teaching staff.* Who are they and how long have they taught or been in leadership? How long have they taught or been in leadership *at that school*?
- *Staff meetings.* Do staff members meet in departments, grade-level, or interdisciplinary learning communities? How often do they meet?
- *How staff use data.* How do teachers get their classroom and schoolwide data? What is the schoolwide plan for analyzing and using data?
- *How staff approach literacy.* What is the school's adopted literacy model? Are all teachers familiar with the model?
- *Staff views of instructional coaching.* What does the staff know about the instructional coaching model that the principal wants to implement?

Gathering these data may require some digging, but they can be very helpful as you think through your coaching strategy and define how you will initiate your work. School-profile data are available from multiple sources. The school itself will house much of the data on students and staff. Look for trends over time. In this regard, many states mandate "school report cards" that often consolidate much of the basic information included in the list. It also may be necessary to look for some older data, especially for information on student performance by grade and subject matter. These data are often found on the state Department of Education website, which typically maintains aggregate information on statewide student testing results for several years.

These data can help you position yourself in your new role. Not all of this information is equally important, but the more you know, the better prepared you are for the job. Even if you are currently working in the school where you will coach, do not take these data for granted. After all, as a teacher, your goals and interests may not have been the same as they are now as a coach.

There are many ways to store the data you collect, such as online programs similar to teacher grading programs, Google Docs, or a good old-fashioned three-ring notebook. Just make sure that whatever storage method you choose is secure. Regardless of the repository, organize the information so it will best inform how you support teachers. If you work with grade-level teachers, organize the data to reflect those cohorts; if you use an online digital tool, organize the data according to the elements used with that tool. It's not unusual for coaches to struggle with keeping organized notes on their work with teachers; but once you nail down a system, the rewards for taking the time to maintain such records will prove critical to your success.

Meeting With the School Leader and the Leadership Team

We cannot stress enough the importance of meeting with the school leader or leadership team to set supportive parameters for instructional coaching. Often these meetings are not easy to schedule. Making time for a serious discussion about coaching may not be high on the list of things the school leader has to do. That said, do what you can to convene this meeting before the school year begins. In a perfect world, it is an opportunity for the coach and the school leader to identify a vision of instructional coaching and share that vision with the staff before implementation.

Be well prepared for the meeting. Show the school leader and the leadership team that you have thought about how you can best do the work of the instructional coach. This is where the homework pays off.

Meetings with school leaders seem to begin in one of several ways (which is why it is so important to be prepared). In some instances, the school leader has a very particular view of what the instructional coach should do. That view may or may not coincide with your understanding of the role. For example, the school leader may want you to be her eyes and ears in the field. She may want you to help with teacher evaluations or observations, may want you to work with "weak teachers" only (as defined by the school leader), or only teachers in one subject area or grade level. If you become defined in these ways, you have significantly compromised your opportunity as an instructional coach. You have "bought" an agenda; you have not set it. This is the time for you to share with the administrator how coaching works most effectively; it is your best chance to help the administrator understand that instructional coaching is not a deficit model and all staff members reside in a community of learning and practice, making struggling teachers empowered and good teachers great! You can paint a detailed picture of all the ways coaches contribute to improving all teachers' practice. You can explain how crucial it is for coaching to be a confidential, nonevaluative process. You may not convince the administrator on every point, but if you have prepared well, you have a real chance to negotiate the role and an opportunity to shape the administrator's understanding of the coaching framework. Of course, the most desirable scenario is one where the coach and the administrator collectively problem-solve and create both the definition and appropriate deliverables.

This is not to say that you will be able to do whatever you want. The meeting with the school leader is simply your best opportunity to influence how that person thinks about your role. The conversation should not be adversarial. Yes, the school leader has the last word, but most are interested and willing to have you *describe the ways in which you can be most effective in helping the school meet its student learning goals*. If you have built an effective case on paper, you have a good chance of making it a reality. If you have carefully and thoughtfully outlined your view of the role, you are poised to help your school leader support your perspective. If you have not, you might end up with less leverage and little leeway in defining and conducting your coaching. Remember, instructional coaching is situational. You can help the school leader understand the potential for schoolwide success and craft a successful plan.

Once you have met with the school leader, you should prepare a summary that you both can use as you move into the school year. Even if you did not arrange a meeting before the actual start of school, do the preparation. Under any circumstances, you will need your case statement and more than a job description in hand if you want to actively engage the school community.

In addition to discussing your role and how instructional coaching can help achieve the schoolwide plans for improvement, discuss when you will share the information about instructional coaching with the faculty. Remember, a coach and a principal standing side-by-side to discuss the schoolwide plans for improvement, student growth, and teacher professional development demonstrates a shared vision for success. This can only happen, however, after the coach and the principal meet to ensure they are on the same page and will work together to increase student engagement and student learning.

Preparing For the First Staff Meeting and Introducing Instructional Coaching

Most schools hold staff meetings on or around the first day of school. This is an important opportunity to start on the right foot. Request a few minutes on the agenda, recognizing that you are not trying to lay out a plan at this point; you are just trying to introduce the role of instructional coaching and help the staff see that you are ready to engage collaboratively with them. Your job is to build awareness and share your goals of helping the school meet its target. Notice that the focus is on achieving the schoolwide goals of improving student learning, not on how you, as the coach, will improve teaching. This point is critical. Coaches are not experts with all the answers, but rather practitioners who want to help the school meet its targeted areas of growth. You want everyone to know that you have met with the school leader and the leadership team. You want them to know that you will work with them and create large- and small-group professional learning opportunities and also offer one-on-one, nonevaluative, confidential support that will be generated from the needs assessment. The goal is for teachers to leave the meeting feeling that you will be out and about as much as possible, working individually and collectively on things that matter to *them*. (See Figure 8.2 for a sample of an introductory staff presentation.)

Assessing Needs and Writing an Action Plan

Needs assessments and action plans are common in the business world. They provide direction and purpose. Equally important, they are subject to iterative review and revision. As such, these are valuable tools for instructional coaches, administrators, and teachers. The needs assessment is an opportunity to meet with others and ask their advice, and by so doing, spot opportunities for intervention, involvement, and collaboration. You can create a short survey to see what kinds of professional development are of interest to groups of teachers. Here is how Ellen approached this task.

Ellen Prepares for Her Coaching Role

I was notified of my new coaching role two months before the school year ended. The staff knew that the school had adopted a new plan and would reassign a teacher to become the instructional coach. Before the appointment, the leadership staff met with focus groups of teachers to talk about instructional coaching and their ideas of how that would help them achieve their schoolwide goals. Although a teacher in the building before becoming the coach, I was not aware of all the initiatives implemented in the school because the staff were divided by committee and seemingly isolated from one other.

Before the school year ended, I was able to convene three groups: two staff member groups and one parent group. The goal was to meet as separate groups and then come together to share ideas and our collective thinking. Student participation would occur throughout the year, especially with older students who could describe the "way things were" as compared to "now." Each group was asked the same questions:

1. What programs, courses, and extracurricular activities are well attended, create a culture of belonging in the school, and are supported by staff and parents?

2. What do you think students like the most about the things you mentioned?

3. When you review schoolwide data, where are the gaps in grade level or subject area data?

4. What kind of "interventions" or academic supports has the school implemented over the last few years to address some of the above-mentioned gaps?

5. Where are students most successful in school? What kind of programs help students become more successful? What do these programs have in common?

6. What one thing would you like to see that would help students and staff take ownership of their learning and become more successful learners?

This was a solid start. We met several times before June and collected our thoughts, our data, our wish list, and our to-do lists. Then I went around to most faculty members and asked some of the same questions. I wanted their voices to be heard as well. They were willing to offer tidbits of information and their help to move things along. From those lists, we prioritized the needs and established some goals that would help us strengthen the things that needed support and build on the things that were already going in the right direction. This list was shared with all of the teachers early in the new school year.

Figure 8.2 Sample Introductory Staff Presentation

Good morning/afternoon.

Thank you for allowing me the opportunity to introduce a new approach to help us meet our goals here at _____. We are always looking for ways to improve teaching and learning, and this year the school has decided to implement instructional coaching as a way of providing personalized professional development to support your practice. I have been identified as the instructional coach to work with you and administrators. [If new to the school, briefly describe credentials and experience.]

Let me share my definition of an instructional coach. An instructional coach is a practitioner whose role is to collaborate with teachers and administrators to introduce changes in practice that will improve student learning. Conversations between the coach and teachers are nonevaluative and confidential. They take place one-on-one or in small groups. An important aspect of my role as a coach is to make certain that all teachers have a chance to engage in professional development that they feel will help them be more effective. For me, instructional coaching happens when staff members meet regularly to talk about teaching and learning. Coaching is intended to help ensure that teachers have time to reflect on their practice. I will try to make these ongoing conversations routine, deliberate, and focused, respecting each teacher's customs and traditions. My role is to help you succeed with your students.

Although you may be familiar with the idea of coaching—it is common with athletes, performing artists, and business executives—this is new for us. And while I've been named instructional coach, please know that we are teaching colleagues and all members in a community of learning and practice. As the year begins, I'll come around and talk with you about my role and how we can work together. In the meantime, please feel free to contact me via my mailbox, my e-mail (xxxxxx@xxxxxxxxxxx), by phone, or stop by and see me in room xxx. If I am out and about, please leave a note for me in the room. I look forward to exploring ways in which we might work together to meet your teaching and learning objectives.

As a result of this experience, a top-10 "hit list" was identified for planning sessions:

1. Form a committee to start the work. Keep it small and easy to manage, but identify a core group of people (insiders—e.g., district and school staff; and outsiders—e.g., parents and community leaders) who are experienced in data collection and analysis.

2. Design an action plan with benchmarks and important due dates; post the plan where the teachers' mailboxes are located.

3. Create a "suggestion box" and place it in a visible place for staff members to drop in their concerns and ideas for improvements.

4. Collect the information, create a list, and then go back to the committee for prioritizing the concerns, ideas, and needs.

5. Decide what data tools are useful to the kinds of data that will be collected.

6. Look at these four areas: organization, curriculum, instruction, and research. How do these areas affect student learning and teacher performance?

7. Align technology with the schoolwide vision for student achievement.

8. Identify root causes—that is, why is this happening?

9. Generate professional development opportunities that are aligned to the school district's priorities and student achievement gaps.

10. Review, readjust, and realign goals.

....

Whether you meet with individual teachers or convene groups to assess needs, there are many factors to consider as you begin to plan your work, including the following:

- If instructional coaching is new to this school, how will we tell the staff about it and how coaches are integral to educator effectiveness?
- If instructional coaching is not new, how can we collaborate to follow up and build on the previous year's successes?
- How will we begin to work together, honoring each teacher's voice and choice?
- How do we work together to co-plan a sustainable professional learning proposal so that the opportunities to nourish our collective and individual growth are deliberate, persistent, and systemic?
- How do we continue to build awareness that the more colleagues work and learn together, the more their students (and each other) will benefit?

Multiple examples of needs-assessment templates are available on the Internet, ranging from simple to complex. Many school districts must conduct assessments to qualify for state or federal funds for particular programs. Check to see if your school jurisdiction has an established format. Don't reinvent the wheel!

What is critical is that the coach and the principal feel comfortable with the plan. Whenever things seem to be off track, steps should be taken to move back to the intentions and purposes outlined in the plan. Although action plans should identify the tasks or action steps, who is responsible for completing those tasks, what resources the responsible party needs to complete the tasks, and the timeline for completion, the plans should allow for some flexibility as well. Certainly circumstances can necessitate changes. In fact, change may be welcomed because it shows that careful consideration was given to the goals and how they were accomplished. When that happens, adjustments must be made to re-assess and re-evaluate the blueprints for change. The plan serves as a framework—a commitment by the coach, with the school leader's support, to deliver certain services, using research-based strategies to move the school toward clear, desired outcomes. When and if the goals change, so do the services and delivery. All of those changes guide practices and strategies so that the intended outcomes are met.

Scheduling

Obtaining teachers' schedules is important because you need to know when and where you can reach them. Try to establish a model schedule for yourself, recognizing that you probably will change it at least a few times. For example, maybe you will try and work with 1st grade teachers on Monday, 2nd grade on Tuesday, and so on. Or, if you happen to work between two buildings, Monday and Tuesday in Building 1, Wednesday and Thursday in Building 2, and Friday wherever there is demand. It is not possible to get all of this settled at the start, but you should have at least a tentative plan so you can prepare your work with teachers, even knowing that the plan may change according to teachers' needs. You must be intentional and flexible at the same time. Remember, you may not have your own classroom papers to review, but you will be planning and preparing to work with teachers across all content areas. And you want to know when professional development time is scheduled so you can become part of those agendas. Again, the important thing is to be visible and show your ability to meet a variety of needs and interests among the school faculty.

The Rollout: Marketing Your Message

Although you might hope that teachers will beat a path to your doorstep, our experience suggests that often the opposite is true. Generate positive buzz by distributing flyers or sending an occasional e-mail blast, in accordance with school policy. Get your contact information in as many public places as you can. Many will be wary, no matter what you say or how much you assure them that your interactions will be nonevaluative and confidential. Some will resent your arrival. If you are not known to all or most of the teachers, you need to build relationships and gather support by showing what you can do. Provide mini professional development opportunities for small groups of teachers and then offer to demonstrate or model those strategies and techniques in classrooms. If you have your own classroom, invite teachers into your room to watch how you implement a particular practice. Keeping communication enthusiastic and open will chip away at hesitancy.

A core decision for the rollout of instructional coaching is figuring out the process. One-on-one coaching is one of the most challenging kinds of coaching, and although it should be a primary objective, it is often not the first coaching activity with colleagues. As we have noted before, small-group or whole-school professional development often leads to the one-on-one conversations. From the more generic professional development sessions, coaches can begin the *before* conversations, ask critical questions, and begin to build a personalized plan for co-teaching or modeling with individual teachers. Recognize that at the beginning, even well-planned small-group activities may be poorly attended. Early on, you may rely on your friends, and they may comprise all or most of your participants. Do not be discouraged. Schedule programs closely aligned with the school's needs and priorities and teachers' interests, and that give you an opportunity to showcase your skills.

Remember, as part of the needs assessment you have surveyed or interviewed teachers to find out their professional development interests. Small-group PD topics are best generated when the staff make suggestions about their own needs and then the sessions are designed accordingly. Staff members are more likely to be fully engaged in the process and content of professional development when they have a voice. Interviewing staff members and brainstorming ideas about schoolwide and individual needs ensures that the ideas are relevant, tied to teacher practice, and connected to statewide initiatives that affect the teachers. The most important thing is to be a presence and receptive to all ideas. Although it is highly desirable to encourage teachers to think of you as a one-on-one resource, that understanding comes about only by building trust, which takes time. Do not oversell yourself. Find your voice by identifying a community and build out from there. Your first few months may be a test of your ability to figure out what matters most to the staff at your school and to develop your instructional coaching around what you learn.

How Ellen Reached New Colleagues

As a new coach, I could not walk into a teacher's room and immediately expect the teacher to work with me. I decided that approaching the staff with a series of short instructional "spurts" or mini professional learning sessions to help teachers fill their toolbox could create a strong environment where learning took place multiple times a day/week/month, developed my credibility, and ultimately helped me begin to schedule some meaningful one-on-one coaching interactions.

I started with bimonthly 20–30 minute "hot spots" where teachers could float into the room and participate in the sessions. The key was that I offered the same session multiple times throughout the same day so that my colleagues could participate whenever they had their planning period. More than once, I provided the same session two days in a row for those who missed the previous day's session.

I facilitated the sessions initially, but after a few months, a few of my colleagues co-planned and co-facilitated the sessions with me. It was thrilling to see how many one-on-one conversations were generated from these small-group mini lessons. I quickly learned that if I offered to demonstrate in their classes the same strategies that I modeled in the sessions, my teaching colleagues were more apt to collaborate with me.

Summing Up

Whether you are new to coaching or it is new to your school—or even if you and the school are veterans at this—certain steps need to be taken to ensure that the coaching plan accomplishes what it sets out to do. These include a needs assessment, a plan of action, early conversations with the school leadership and the staff about the role, and carefully designed rollout strategies. Organize to take advantage of any early momentum you may achieve, but remember that introducing instructional coaching requires perseverance. And if you begin and end each day by answering the questions *What am I doing as a coach to help teachers change and improve their practice?* and *What am I doing as a coach to help teachers improve student engagement and outcomes?*, you will succeed.

One Story of Patience and Perseverance

One coach, Joanne Custer, takes changes in her careers totally in stride—moving from positions as a lending assistant for the banking industry to an English language arts teacher to a reading specialist to an instructional coach. It is in the last role that she advises some restraint. "Feel your way," she says.

Responding to perceived needs has taken Custer on this varied journey. She became a reading specialist, for example, because so many students who were enrolled at her comprehensive career technology high school lacked sufficient reading skills. Similarly, she moved into an instructional coach's position because she wanted to influence teaching and learning in a different way.

Even though Custer became a coach in the school where she also had been a teacher, she needed to move cautiously. Her initial support for the teachers mostly involved finding information they wanted and doing "data walks" in classrooms to learn what would be helpful. Sometimes she would tell teachers, "I've done this before, so why don't I model it, then you give me feedback." By doing that, she says, "they have input and control over the strategy."

Custer began her instructional coaching by working with individual teachers whom she knew well enough to be invited into their classrooms. Her service delivery has become the BDA cycle for coaching. "It lends itself nicely to not only increased knowledge of instruction," she says, "but also allows the relationships between a coach and teachers to grow." In addition to one-on-one coaching, she has created a lively portfolio of group work with teachers such as book studies, 20-minute "Lunch 'N' Learns" every Monday, and Tweak of the Week, which offers new information or ideas. The instructional coaching "is totally based on what interests we have cultivated in our school," she says. "What we do here might not work in another setting."

One advantage Custer enjoys is the total support of her principal. "She has gone through the professional development for coaches herself, and we work together to plan professional development for the whole staff," Custer says. The principal understands the importance of confidentiality in instructional coaching, she adds.

In addition to her support from the principal, Custer relies on different kinds of networks. One is right in the school: there are two other instructional coaches for the 1,000-student high school—for math/data analysis and for technology. The three coaches work together cohesively, especially on strategies to reach teachers reluctant to use their support. Two years after becoming an instructional coach, Custer discovered the Pennsylvania Institute for Instructional Coaching (PIIC), which provides her with a wide network of other coaches for sharing and advice.

Through the networks and the intensive mentoring of PIIC, Custer tries to improve the skills she thinks are necessary to being a good instructional coach—listening well, flexibility, positive approaches, research knowledge, and understanding how adults learn best. The focus on adult learning, she says, "has allowed me to really fine-tune my questioning techniques, because adults do not want to hear lectures."

Her instructional coaching role also has led to further higher education. Because of the statewide interest in coaching, several state campuses are offering courses that collectively make up a new instructional coaching endorsement. Custer is enrolled in this program while continuing to listen to, support, and expand the horizons of the teachers in her school. In her experience, she needed four years of coaching at the school before she felt she was making a real difference. When the coaching team started, about 10 percent of the staff accepted coaching support; now, about 60 percent are involved. Custer keeps a log of the activities and can document that the coaching is having a successful impact. Teachers no longer say they are hampered by students who can't read, she says. "I've given them skills to help struggling readers. They are empowered."

9

Coaches at Work:
Growing Into the Coaching Role

Instructional coaching is a relationship between professional colleagues aimed at improving instruction to meet student needs. When implemented effectively, both the instructional coach and teacher grow in professional knowledge and skills.

—Dr. Brian Toth, Superintendent

After coaches have established a scope of work, met with school leaders and teachers, and begun assessing needs, many questions emerge. Whereas the last chapter focused on getting started as a coach, this one looks more closely at moving a practice forward. The chapter begins by looking at the continuum of adopters—from teachers who want to engage with coaches, to teachers who are disinterested or unwilling to interact with coaches. Then, after a discussion of the terms "situational" (referring to the uniqueness of each coaching interaction depending on the circumstances and situation) and "deliberate" (referring to intentional time and planning for coaching), the chapter turns to the evolution of practice, exploring another continuum—how coaches move from "light" to "heavy" coaching, intensifying the breadth and depth of their practice over time. In this context, coach self-assessment is discussed. In its entirety, this chapter looks at the critical considerations that can help coaches achieve an effective practice.

Finding a Constituency: The Continuum of Adopters

As we have noted, some schools and some teachers are receptive to the idea of coaching; others less so. Coaches have to work their market, just like any other service provider, and find a welcoming constituency. We have identified some keys to help break down potential barriers and get the momentum going.

115

Start With the Willing

Teachers are among the few practitioners who do not routinely practice with each other. They typically stand alone in their classroom, doors closed, with few opportunities to talk to each other, let alone collaborate. So coaches need to actively build awareness about the potential value of instructional coaching; they need to begin by cultivating strong relationships, collaborating on a regular basis, and demonstrating that every teacher has some expertise to share even though they are not experts. Not every teacher recognizes what makes for effective instruction, so coaches need to help them become reflective practitioners and think about what they do, why they do it, and how they do it.

Because of the limited networking time available to teachers, a coach's experiences and skill set are not always recognized. Teachers often are fearful, uncomfortable, and unfamiliar with anyone other than an administrator coming into the classroom. Remember, a teacher's schedule rarely includes time to visit other classrooms or to plan with other teachers. In fact, a visit without appropriate planning is often unproductive and can be misconstrued as an administrative directive. The coach must be careful to set the stage for a visit with proper preplanning and collaboration. The planning is a collective problem-solving endeavor and not one that should be muddied with a "snapshot in time" experience. For a teacher who has not experienced instructional coaching, a predictable reaction is, "If I don't know what you expect of me, how can I be comfortable enough to let you see me possibly make a mistake?" One coach's experience illustrates this point.

From Zero to Three to More

One of the coaches we worked with told us that in the beginning of her school's coaching initiative, she was sure that everyone would open their doors and work with her. After all, they were all part of the faculty who regularly vented that they needed more professional development to help them get better at their craft. The coach knew that the teachers all wanted what was best for their students even though they may not have agreed on how to get there. So imagine the coach's surprise when she was "reintroduced" to the staff as the new instructional coach and asked how many people would "allow" her to come into their rooms and support their instructional needs. No hands were raised!

She realized that she needed to break down the fear of having someone visit classrooms in a nonevaluative way and build awareness of how effective instructional coaching works, both at the same time. She began planning small networking opportunities where colleagues could meet together and talk about how to make the learning more effective for all the students. These kinds of conversations centered around stressful questions like "Why do I need an instructional coach" or "How can the coach and I work together to implement effective instructional practices so that our students can grow as learners?"

It wasn't easy, but here's how the coach bridged the gap. The coach asked three friends on staff if she could model something in their classes so she could get acclimated to modeling in front of students who were not her own and build her credibility. They agreed and decided that the coach would model the same thing in all three classes (this was doable because they were all 11th grade English language arts teachers). The planning would take place in the teacher's cafeteria so others could hear the conversation. Each teacher agreed to collect the same data at the time of the visit and then they would meet again in the cafeteria to talk about what happened. Each of the teachers then agreed that they would co-facilitate a mini professional development session with the coach for other teachers using the same evidence-based literacy practices following the coach's modeling session. As the coach hoped, the teachers spread the word about the co-planning, modeling, and nonevaluative debriefing to build the awareness of how instructional coaching works to help teachers implement effective instructional practices.

Break the Ice

Coaches can break the ice in many ways. Here are some common approaches:

- Talk about instructional coaching, one-on-one and in small groups, as a way of addressing schoolwide and continuous improvement, not just in terms of an individual's practice.
- Focus on why teachers may be reluctant to work with the coach. Some teachers probably do not understand the role of the coach or why the coach has become the coach in the first place: *Why her and not me?* Ego can get in the way. When teachers realize that the coaching, at its core, is about students, more doors open.
- Understand the kinds of questions that come up for teachers when offered the opportunity to work with a coach. *Does that mean I don't know how to teach or*

that my own skills are insufficient? Does it mean that I don't understand my content as well as someone else (like the coach) does? Does it mean I'm not good at what I do? These kinds of questions are typical for teachers to ask (or think) when an instructional coach is hired. The coach needs to make clear to teachers that it's not about what's wrong with a teacher's instruction; it's all about how to promote effective practices. That is, the coach needs to create an environment where teachers are not afraid to try new things and make mistakes, knowing that someone is there to help them learn from their experiences.

- Find emissaries of goodwill, or champions, and begin to co-plan and co-facilitate with them. If staff members see the collective strength of two or more individuals collaborating with mutual respect, this sets an example that helps to project a positive image to the staff, especially if the coaching relationship involves a respected veteran. It takes time, but teachers eventually will understand that the coach is there to help, not hinder, their practice.

- Use schoolwide data to gain access to classrooms. The coach can help teachers understand the data available to them and talk about how to address what they see to the benefit of students. Drilling down into individual classroom data can be intimidating; coaches need to tread lightly at the outset. Using the schoolwide improvement plan, analyze schoolwide data and look for areas ripe for improvement. This can be a way to show teachers that the coach is focused on improving outcomes for the whole school and that working with every teacher can contribute to that collective goal.

- As noted earlier, start with the willing, then build relationships by "nagging and nurturing, patting and pushing" those who are reticent. The most resistant teachers may be those who lack the confidence to admit they have things to learn or that they can share with their colleagues; they may be afraid that they've been teaching "wrong" for several years. Or they just don't know what they don't know!

- Design small-group and whole-staff professional development that meets a recognized need and interest of a number of teachers. Offer coaching around issues of practice that have broad appeal and ask colleagues if they can co-plan and co-facilitate the sessions. It is amazing what happens when a colleague is part of the process.

Trust is an important element of the equation. Building support, even among the willing, requires that teachers feel comfortable in their relationships. Coaches need to begin with a plan for building awareness of how instructional coaching works. Such a plan would create "credible" moments when the coach can help groups rather than individuals and promote a process for identifying schoolwide needs for professional development. This can only be accomplished by approaching every teacher and giving that teacher voice and choice, thereby building trust, establishing confidentiality, and affirming that the coach does not have a direct line to the principal and is not the principal's eyes and ears. This is easier said than done. Remember, actions speak louder than words, so the coach must maintain an absolute commitment to nonevaluative and confidential support and work to persuade every teacher that this is what has been negotiated with the school principal.

The best way to develop trust is to build staff awareness of coaching goals and objectives and reaffirm the importance of confidentiality and the integrity of instructional coaching throughout the year. Coaches should never fall into the trap of sharing what they have seen or experienced in working with individual teachers. Even sharing information about a great lesson or how easy it is to work with some teachers is a sure way to diminish the coach's ability to reach all teachers. On the other hand, if an administrator asks about what's happening in a particular classroom, a coach cannot be insubordinate and not respond. Rather than making an evaluative comment about a classroom visit, it is much better for the coach to say to the principal, "The teachers would like you to see firsthand what their students are doing in class." It's also helpful to remind administration of the parameters around which coaches must operate.

Coaches should ask teachers what they know about coaching, what they want to know, and how they think coaching can help promote student achievement and schoolwide improvement. Coaches should spend time at the beginning of the year gathering feedback and just talking about how instructional coaching can benefit students through their teachers' access to enhanced classroom practices, and revisit these opportunities throughout the year.

If coaches show what they have to offer and build trusting relationships with teachers, teachers will come to understand what coaching can offer and will not think of the coach as a "spy" for the school leadership. The following account reinforces this point.

....

A Coach's Regret

Tuesdays are my days for classroom visitations with the 7th grade science team. The experiments are always challenging and engaging to the students. They clearly love the idea of making things "explode" and guessing when that will happen. Mrs. Lopez is always quick to let the students experiment and make predictions. Her students are focused and quite accustomed to the procedures necessary for these experiments.

Today's class followed the route Mrs. Lopez and I discussed in our *before* meeting. Her goals were clearly explained and attainable by all the students, even those who had some learning challenges; they were partnered with stronger students, making it clear that Mrs. Lopez really knew her students. It was obvious the students understood the directions and the purpose of the lesson when, at the end of the class, Mrs. Lopez gave a quick "ticket out the door" activity that checked for understanding and let her know how to proceed the next day. I stayed after the class for a few minutes to see how the students responded to the exit task.

Walking through the hallway, I was reminded how Mrs. Lopez set clear expectations for her students, and they knew it, too. They felt energized at understanding the components of the experiment and were able to show Mrs. Lopez that they were successful that day. They were chatting about the class as they walked to their next period. While still thinking about this terrific class, I ran into the principal.

Principal Scott said to me, "I was looking for you. Which classroom did you visit and how did it go?" Still invigorated, I blurted out, "I was with Mrs. Lopez. What a great class lesson! Mrs. Lopez's class was interactive; the students were all engaged; and her instructional delivery really hit the appropriate core standards. The students left certainly understanding the content."

The next day I went back to Mrs. Lopez for our *after* meeting. At the door, Mrs. Lopez stopped me and told me she was no longer interested in working with me. This totally confused me; we had been working together all year. But Mrs. Lopez refused to engage in conversation. Finally, after much pleading to explain what was wrong, Mrs. Lopez admitted that she was offended, outraged, and shocked that I had shared an evaluation of her class to the principal. I was dumbfounded. "How can you be upset? I only shared the wonderful job you did with the students and how well the students responded to you."

"Yes, you did," replied Mrs. Lopez. "But you constantly remind us that our work with you is confidential, yet you immediately communicated what happened in my class with the principal. That breached all confidentiality, and frankly, I've lost trust in our relationship and working with you. Please do not expect me to make time to meet with you to discuss my practice." I tried to repair this relationship over the course of the year. Although the teacher still participated in a variety of coach-led activities, I was never able to completely repair our relationship.

....

Divulging classroom information in a way that places value on the work is, obviously, evaluative and must be left to the principal or the principal's designee. In response to the principal, the coach should have simply replied, "I was working with the science department. Students really seem to enjoy conducting experiments and discovering new facts. Visiting these science classrooms would give you an idea of what they are doing in class."

Overcoming Resistance

Making believers out of skeptics is all about building credibility. One thing is certain: instructional coaches cannot persuade teachers that they have something to offer just by "chatting them up." Credibility is about "show me." The only way to turn around a skeptic is to engage in professional development that is valued by the community. This is especially the case when a colleague has become a senior among peers and is now the coach. *Yesterday, the coach was my peer asking for my advice; today, my peer is now the coach trying to give me some advice.* For many, this is not an easy transition.

Coaches should take their needs assessments seriously. Persuade those who are disinterested by implementing programs that speak to the staff's perceived needs. There is no logic in trying to coax teachers into relationships they do not believe will benefit them. Use professional development as the hook. Coaches get the attention of teachers when teachers hear and see that they have something to gain by becoming involved. In fact, if the coach also teaches (not our recommendation), she can select a time and invite colleagues into her classroom to demonstrate some instructional practices. This effort goes a long way. For one thing, it shows that the coach is willing to be vulnerable and open her own classroom for others to visit and give feedback; second, it shows good faith that the coach is not an expert and is willing to share new ideas; and third, it demonstrates the power of the BDA process that feedback and reflection change practice as a result of the conversation that follows the visit.

Every coach worries over how to engage reluctant teachers. In fact, there is no one way to convince every teacher that coaches have something to offer them. There are, however, some strategies that can encourage them to keep an open mind.

1. *Make use of the research you gathered.* Share it with teachers to show them the great benefit of coaching across various fields, such as performing arts, athletics, business, and weight loss.

....

How Ellen Made the Case for a Tough Crowd

When I first started coaching in a school that had not implemented a coaching model previously, I knew that there would be some dissenters—not because they didn't like me but because they were afraid that I would tell them that they were teaching incorrectly—or worse, using inappropriate teaching methods. I recognized that I needed to show them that coaching in other domains was effective and ask them how coaching could help them achieve their schoolwide goals. So I asked some simple questions: "How many of you have had any kind of private lessons?" Several raised their hands. I proceeded: "Were they group or individual lessons?" Several shared their experiences with private voice lessons, piano lessons, weight-loss counseling, or golf lessons with a pro. Then I asked about group lessons. Several said they played on various athletic teams that were coached or practiced in a choir group. Next question: "How many of you had both individual and group lessons for the same coached activity, such as weight-loss support, swimming teams, tennis lessons, art lessons?" Not as many had experienced both. Then I asked, "Which kind of support provided personal attention, the group tennis lessons or one-on-one with a tennis pro; the group weight-loss weigh-in and discussion or a private one-on-one consultation?" They all agreed that individual tennis lessons with a pro yielded a more personal approach to skills building. The same was true for weight-loss support and all the other activities. Finally, I asked how many ever did any tutoring or had been tutored during their student days. Several said they, or their children, were tutored. I asked if they thought their children had more personalized support when they were tutored in a group or when the tutor worked with their children one-on-one. Everyone said they wanted their children tutored one-on-one so that their questions could be answered and their weaknesses strengthened.

That was the end of our first conversation. They knew what I was trying to show, and they laughed at the end of the meeting. But this is not a fairy tale ending; just because they understood where I was going with the conversation, it didn't mean that they all asked me to work with them. That took a little longer for some colleagues, less for others. Either way, I always went back to the conversation about group lessons or one-on-one. Why was that support successful in order to go from good to great?

....

2. *Recognize and work with the early adopters and let the good word spread.*

3. *Wherever possible, co-plan, co-facilitate, and debrief with others to show that you are all members in a community of learning.* You may be an instructional coach, but that is not because you know more than anyone else. You do, however, know about adult learning and will provide every opportunity for collaboration and learning together. The following coach's experience is a good example of this.

....

Learning Together

My first one-on-one visit to a former colleague's classroom was daunting. Did she think I was supposed to be an expert? I certainly didn't think so, and I knew I had to draw all my strength from the credibility I had as a colleague. I was afraid the teacher would ask me something to which I didn't know the answer. I tried to put myself in the place of a student who asks a question and the teacher doesn't know the answer. It was then that I remembered what my cooperating teacher told me during my student teaching years. Mr. Muncy's advice was "Listen to the students' answers. First give them time to answer something you asked and then give them time to ask you a question. If you don't know the answer, admit it and compliment the student on thinking about something you didn't. Ask the student to actually pursue the answer and share what he or she discovered the next day in class. That way, you'll show the students that everyone is a learner and that the mark of an educated person is the desire to learn from one another, not just from someone who thinks he or she knows all the answers. If you are not a learner, your students cannot be learners either." It was great advice and something I thought about over and over that year.

By the end of the year, I had become very comfortable admitting what I didn't know and invited all of my teaching colleagues to continually ask the kinds of questions that demonstrated their ability to dig deeper and extend their thinking. This carried over to their students, so that asking questions and inviting teachable moments became the standard. As I modeled through example how I opened up my thinking, they, too, felt comfortable demonstrating how their reasoning and thinking abilities changed; they became more reflective practitioners, which made me more reflective as well.

....

4. *Take a back seat during a meeting; let the teachers talk and share ideas.* You can facilitate by asking some questions and taking notes, but let the teachers' voices be heard.

5. *Recognize that the issue is not about ego.* If a teacher is not willing to collaborate, a coach should try to talk about practice and engage that person in helpful ways. Reluctant teachers do not always understand collaboration. Coaches need to remind their colleagues that the idea of coaching has been around for a long time, and coaches are partners in the learning process. A coach could ask the reluctant teachers if they have ever been coached as a student, then talk about those experiences.

6. *Know when to give people space.* In general, resisters can only be brought along on their own terms. Knocking unannounced at a colleague's door is not the most effective approach. No one wants to be surprised. There must be a grace period, when timing, thinking, and transforming take place. Some coaches overinvest in trying to develop relationships with resistant teachers. Resistance is only overcome by showing *all* teachers that coaching can help improve practice. As noted, focus on working with the more willing teachers, highlight their success, and keep looking for opportunities to work with groups of teachers that include both the interested and the uninterested (recognizing that some will never come to value what is offered). Then let the hesitant teachers come to you.

From Situational to Deliberate Practice

Where are you headed as a coach? That is the ultimate question for most coaches once they settle into their new roles. Many feel bogged down by the mundane yet often enervating daily effort to "keep everyone happy." Provide some instructional resources to one teacher, model for another teacher, help a third teacher look at some formative data, work on a small-group professional development program—the work of coaching starts to look like a series of unconnected actions. And that is what it can become, unless the coach provides some structure.

This is not an unusual challenge, but it calls to mind a singular point: effective coaches are not just responsive to an isolated request. They do not answer every teacher's every request without the benefit of an extended conversation. They plan thoughtfully, with a purpose. Indeed, coaches are often torn in many directions at once. But it is important to remember that they should have a plan for where they are trying to go. Rather than allow situations to totally dominate their work, coaches should design some larger goals. (Remember the action planning!) They should have objectives for the year that they can articulate and periodic milestones to review to see if they are moving toward them. They should have bigger targets for helping all teachers grow—for example, helping all subject area teachers enhance students' writing skills. They may recognize that they need to be responsive to the very different needs of teachers, but they should know where to draw the line.

One coach we worked with struggled with this issue. She had to think about the new emphasis on writing and how to help her teaching colleagues understand how to integrate writing into their classroom routines.

Keeping the Objective in Mind

Several years ago, the thinking about writing in all classes was not as prevalent as it is today. Many teachers did not recognize that students needed multiple times each day to practice writing and that, in fact, those multiple writing opportunities nurtured and matured their students' writing skills so that they could write about what they learned and demonstrate their understanding of content.

The coach showed the teachers both in their one-on-one *before* planning sessions and in small-group professional learning sessions that writing to learn was very effective. She started each session with one thought-provoking question and asked her colleagues to jot their thoughts either in phrases, sentences, or bulleted lists. Then she asked them to turn to their elbow partners and share their thoughts. After sharing with one another, she asked each pair to reveal to the group something new they learned from the response or a question they had that was generated by the response. She expanded that practice each time she met with the teachers to include something a little more challenging via a paragraph about practice or another pertinent topic in their content areas. Each time, she tried to show how reading and writing responses helped form new learning. By the end of the coaching cycle, teachers from many different content areas were routinely implementing this "writing to learn" strategy at the start of each of their classes.

Coaches have a choice about the work they do. They start with the schoolwide goals for improvement and decide how the work can help accomplish those goals. They do not provide every answer. In truly effective coaching, the answers come from the teachers, not the coach. After all, the coach asks the questions and helps the teachers think about their own thinking and rise to their fullest potential, just as teachers help their students rise to their fullest potential. That happens through inquiry, invitation, and risk-free conversations.

Coaches often start out in "situational" mode. They want to please everyone, prove themselves, and win over their doubters. They want to draw interest. They want the principal to feel that they are contributing. They want the needs to define the actions. All this is for the good. But it should not be the whole of their coaching focus. It is equally important for the coach's constituents—teachers and school administrators—to know that their work is deliberate with a direction, a set of particular objectives, and unshakable goals. Once the coach defines the goals, ideally with the help of the teachers and the school leader, the coach can then prioritize and make certain that most of the coaching that is done is aligned with these larger goals. This is not just a matter of survival; it is central to being effective and providing a productive instructional coaching model.

Virtual Support

The educator-centered instructional coaching model emphasizes one-on-one and small-group delivery. That said, we recognize that coaches and their mentors (see Chapter 10 for more about mentors) can benefit from using technology to economize and enhance their capacity to work with teachers. Technology supplements the face-to-face process; it does not replace it.

The jury is still out on the effectiveness of web-based and digital classroom data gathering by coaches. Although these tools may be cost effective and virtual visits may have value, our view is that coaches can only see and feel the "whole" classroom experience by being in the teacher's presence. The data collection process enables the coach to gain insights into how a particular teacher approaches teaching, and it may be facilitated via an electronic approach. This is a useful step before face-to-face collaborative coaching conversations—the "before the *before*" preparation when both parties can use the data to ask probing and clarifying questions about practice.

Digital communications can certainly enhance the coaching experience and create more frequent opportunities to talk. We continually use webinars, wikis, and YouTube channels to support our professional development agendas. We fully appreciate and train coaches to help teachers use a wide variety of digital teaching tools and social media classroom platforms that should be part of every teacher's instructional repertoire. We recognize that e-mail, virtual office hours, Skype, and social media can expedite communications among mentors, coaches, and teachers.

To bridge the infrequent times when coaches can gather and work together, we have designed a website with a plethora of resources and tools including videos, templates, and materials that can help coaches in their practice. Organized topically, it highlights top priorities for coaches: understanding their role and understanding the role of mentors; working effectively in each domain of the educator-centered instructional coaching framework; organizing for one-on-one and small-group coaching; collecting, analyzing, and applying data on student learning; improving literacy across all content areas; and reflective and nonevaluative practice. The website helps practitioners who spend relatively little time together attain a common foundation and have access to the same tools. (See www.instituteforinstructional coaching.org, The Pennsylvania Institute for Instructional Coaching.)

Although we recognize and use a variety of technologies, the essence of our instructional coaching framework is that it is personalized. Although this may seem old-fashioned, we have found that only face-to-face collaboration enables coach and teacher to take full advantage of the BDA cycle. We can support a blended approach, accomplishing the *before* and the *after* phases electronically; but for the *during* phase to be effective, an in-person visit is best. The discussion throughout the *after* is significant and leads to the next *before* conversation. It is here where the alignment of what was planned is weighed against what was delivered and what adjustments in teaching are necessary. A face-to-face conversation gives both parties an opportunity to respond in real time and expand their thinking with questions that might not be so obvious in an electronic message.

Coaches recognize that communication is the lifeline of their practice; but they also know that the limitations of time, energy, and intervening factors can inhibit their ability to keep the conversations flowing and support ongoing. Technology can be a useful tool to make communication and planning easier. One of our colleagues, Ms. O'Brien, found an effective way to keep everyone connected while still providing the face-to-face support her coaching cohort craved.

Staying Connected

In the middle of each week, Ms. O'Brien sent e-mails to her coaching group with the next schedule of biweekly activities—what days and times she or some colleagues were providing mini professional learning sessions with topics generated by her weekly "chats and chews" with staff members at lunch time—or articles about new educational trends that she thought would be useful. Also included in the e-mails was a template where colleagues could ask a question, send a request, or share an article of interest and send it back to her. The requests generated the content for the "Coach's Corner" one-pager that she disseminated monthly, additional professional learning session topics for small-group work, and one-on-one, face-to-face planning sessions.

Additionally, Ms. O'Brien wanted to ensure that she was prepared for the *before* sessions she planned with her teaching colleagues. She sent an e-mail to teachers ahead of each *before* session, asking what kinds of things they wanted to discuss at their meeting. She also took the opportunity to suggest some dates for the *after* session. If a colleague had a specific topic in mind, she pursued the topic and collected information and data aligned with that topic to bring to the meeting. If a colleague wanted to talk about a specific instructional strategy, she would have additional examples of similar instructional strategies that supported the content as well. Collected online, these ideas helped populate the discussions for the *before* planning sessions.

....

We should acknowledge that using technology well requires time and effort. Not every educator is well versed and comfortable in the digital world. We encourage coaches to explore its uses while recognizing that electronic communication serves as a means to foster ongoing face-to-face collaboration in a busy environment, not as a substitute for it. If coaches rely too much on contact via digital devices, they maintain a distance that might keep the relationship somewhat superficial and impede progress.

This observation leads us to an approach that may help coaches think through the longer term. It involves mapping levels of intensity of coaching, a key measure of coaching progress and also the currency of self-assessment.

Levels of Intensity: Diving Deeper into Coaching Relationships

To help coaches become more deliberate, strategic, and more systematic in practice, we use a set of measures that we call "Levels of Intensity." These levels cover a variety of coaching functions that are described by three levels of practice, each involving progressively greater depth of the coaching relationship. The levels become a fairly complex formulation in at least three ways: within levels with a multitude of teachers, across levels with the same teacher, and across multiple levels with multiple teachers.

First, in a given school, the coach often works with several teachers in varying degrees of intensity. For example, some teachers need to move more slowly with more support in some areas, while others are ready to roll from the onset. Coaches need to nag and nurture so that they are moving teachers along to promote effective instructional practices driven by their needs. It is not the same for each teacher. For example, opening a dialogue and introducing one teacher to the BDA cycle of consultation (Level 1) while simultaneously engaging another teacher in deep discussions that get to the heart of the BDA cycle (Level 3) can and does occur. Second, a coach can work with the same teacher in multiple levels depending on the nature of the work. A coach may work with Teacher A in Level 1 around that teacher's classroom data. That same teacher, however, might be ready to work with the coach around ways to facilitate grade-level meetings to discuss their literacy model, which is more involved and resides in Level 2. The coaching level ebbs and flows across the functions. No one expects the coach to work across all three levels with every teacher, but the objective over time is to move both the teachers' and coach's practices forward to ensure the implementation of effective instructional practices.

As shown in Figure 9.1, the Levels of Intensity are part of a continuum of practice. As coaches grow on the job, they become increasingly skilled at helping teachers sharpen their instructional skills and delving deeper into their practice. These levels are important benchmarks, indicators of progress that help coaches understand their contribution to their school's mission.

Level 1 coaching is both structured and informal. The conversations are not vague; coaches prepare and ensure that the communication is not overwhelming or daunting. The activities described in this level are those that establish trusting relationships and build awareness of introductory coaching interactions. Coaches introduce the BDA cycle of consultation conceptually, focusing on small-group work rather than one-on-one conferencing. They build a shared vision by targeting the schoolwide improvement plans, data, state standards, and how coaching helps scaffold that learning for teachers. Coaches continue to elicit responses from colleagues about identifying the needs, goals, and distinct areas of needed support.

Level 2 coaching consultations involve a more hands-on approach. The support is more directed and moves the conversation to the individual, expanding to include focus areas, data analysis, and reflective practice. Coaches and teachers collaborate to develop sustainable, ongoing professional learning and personalized support focusing on the teacher's learning needs necessary to move student performance upward.

Figure 9.1 Examples of Levels of Intensity for Instructional Coaches

Level 1: Informal; helps to develop relationships
- Building awareness of the BDA cycle of coaching and the four core elements
- Talking with colleagues confidentially about educator effectiveness and identifying goals for growth, literacy learning, and student needs (identifying issues or needs, setting goals, problem solving)
- Developing and providing materials for/with colleagues
- Helping teachers understand and integrate Common Core State Standards
- Exploring websites for exemplars and using effective instructional strategies
- Participating in professional development activities with colleagues (e.g., conferences, workshops, professional learning opportunities)
- Co-facilitating or participating in study groups, book talks, and other conferences
- Helping teachers understand student assessment data and identifying areas of focus
- Facilitating conversations with teachers about areas of strength and areas of need
- Looking at schoolwide and classroom data
- Providing small-group professional learning opportunities (e.g., PD at faculty meetings)

Level 2: More formal; somewhat more intense; begins to look at areas of need and focus
- Beginning the BDA cycle of instructional coaching (e.g., *before* meetings with teachers)
- Co-planning lessons and identifying appropriate evidenced-based instructional strategies
- Facilitating team meetings (grade level or content level) to discuss student performance, literacy learning, and using data to inform instruction
- Analyzing student work and identifying areas of strength and areas of need
- Interpreting assessment data (helping teachers use results for instructional decision making)
- One-on-one and small-group support for teachers and reflecting "in, on, and about" actions
- Developing professional development presentations for sustainable teacher support

Level 3: Formal, more intense; moves interactions from general to specific
- Co-planning, co-teaching, and debriefing lessons (BDA cycle of instructional coaching)
- Modeling and debriefing lesson design, instructional techniques, integration of technology
- Visiting classrooms and providing feedback to teachers
- Analyzing videotaped lessons where available and appropriate (360° cameras/iPAD)
- Facilitating one-on-one and small-group professional learning and scenario problem solving
- Planning and facilitating nonevaluative lesson study with teachers
- Providing whole-school professional learning (e.g., establishing effective PLCs)

Source: From "Promoting Effective Literacy Instruction: The Challenge for Literacy Coaches," by R. M. Bean, Spring 2004, *The California Reader, 37*(3), pp. 58–63. Copyright 2004 by The California Reading Association. Adapted with permission.

Level 3 coaching conversations move the interactions from the general to the specific. Coaches work more closely with teachers to implement the full BDA cycle of consultation, with more one-on-one conversations and a more detailed, nonevaluative investigation of instructional delivery. The coach and the teacher are more comfortable co-teaching and expand their collaboration to include other colleagues in group settings to review lessons, offer suggestions, and revise their thinking. The give-and-take between coach and teacher is steady and deliberate, moving practice to the community of learners to change the culture of the school. Conversations are professional; co-planning, co-teaching, and reflection are the norm. Although this level may be more challenging, the end result is more noticeable because practice is shared and collective problem solving habitual.

Coaches can use the table in Figure 9.2 to inform how they apply the Levels of Intensity in their practice. The table focuses on the big ideas and shows what implementation looks like for each level of support. Each category is multipurpose; that is, every intensity area—one-on-one, BDA, and so on—can be implemented in multiple ways for each of the teachers the coach supports. For instance, a coach may provide Level 2 support, "Modeling facilitation of effective professional learning opportunities," in mini professional development sessions for several teachers, which might generate a Level 3 form of support with one of those same teachers. The big ideas in the table may shape the coach's action planning. Each level of support influences how the coach provides the detail and can be tweaked to address individual needs.

Levels of Intensity and Self-Assessment

Like other professionals, instructional coaches crave feedback—they want to know how they are doing on the job. Formal evaluation of coaches by supervisors is a way to help coaches reflect on and improve their practice, but coaches can also use the Levels of Intensity to self-assess. Coaches can ask themselves: *How am I doing on each of these functions? Am I progressing toward deeper and more substantial inquiry on each? Do I have a plan that will help me move teaching from one level of intensity to the next on each?* Equally important, in terms of self-assessment, are these two questions:

- What themes and issues have emerged from my work with teachers and how might that affect my future planning?
- What strategies can I use next year that will enhance administrative support for my work as a coach?

Although the specifics of the Levels of Intensity scale may vary, the point is this: Levels of Intensity provide a structure, a planning tool, and a self-assessment opportunity. Coaches can use the self-assessment template (Figure 9.3) to gauge their coaching work.

Figure 9.2 Summary of Levels of Intensity for Instructional Coaches

Intensity Area	Level 1 Informal; helps to develop relationships	Level 2 More formal, somewhat more intense; begins to look at areas of need or focus	Level 3 Formal, more intense; moves interactions from general to specific
One-on-One and Small-Group Meetings	Planning and facilitating meetings with individuals and teams of teachers	Modeling facilitation of effective professional learning opportunities for adult learners through monthly meetings	Providing feedback to teachers on content, process, and format of meetings
BDA Cycle	Building teachers' and administrators' awareness of the BDA cycle of coaching as well as one-on-one and small-group support	Reinforcing the BDA cycle of coaching through modeling and watching the work of teachers	Deepening the BDA cycle through the effective use of clarifying and probing questions; listening for limiting beliefs; facilitating the reframing process; and developing self-awareness of strengths and challenges
Coaches' Networking Meetings	Planning and facilitating networking meetings with teachers	Modeling facilitation of effective professional learning opportunities for adult learners through monthly networking meetings with teachers	Coach and teachers co-planning professional learning activities and agenda items for networking meetings; discussing strategies and arranging classroom visits; collaborating to solve problems and develop plans for implementation
Improving Classroom Practices	Developing and providing materials for teachers to support improved classroom instruction	Modeling the use of evidence-based literacy and other classroom practices that are applicable to all content areas	Providing opportunities for reflective feedback and collective problem solving around using literacy strategies and other classroom practices
Formative and Summative Assessments	Helping teachers differentiate and identify the purposes of formative, summative, benchmark, and diagnostic assessments for students	Creating opportunities for teachers to understand the various kinds of formative and summative data and how to analyze and use the collected data	Supporting teachers to look at data systemically and to use data to implement instructional or curricular changes
State Teacher Evaluation Plan: Teacher Effectiveness Framework (TEF)	Helping staff develop an understanding of a district's teacher effectiveness framework (TEF) and the role of a coach in the process	Providing one-on-one and small-group support to teachers as they identify issues and needs, set goals, solve problems, and navigate the state's teacher effectiveness framework (TEF)	Providing feedback to teachers related to the district's teacher effectiveness framework (TEF) and goals for growth

Figure 9.3 Levels of Intensity Self-Assessment Template (Midyear and End-of-Year Tool)

Intensity Area	Current Level of Intensity (Level 1, 2, or 3 as defined by the LOI document)	What? (What did I do to address this focus area?)	So What? (What impact did my actions have on meeting my objectives?)	Now What? (What do I plan to do going forward?)
Evidence-Based Practices				
Needs Assessment and Continuous Improvement				
Improving Classroom Practices				
Formative and Summative Assessments				

Coaches often worry about how helpful they are to their teaching colleagues. They wonder if they are laying a solid foundation for the instructional coaching process and demonstrating effective practices. They know learning is the ultimate goal and want to ensure that they are doing all they can to provide meaningful support and continue to make a difference in teaching and learning. In this sense, coaches can use the Levels of Intensity table and these additional questions to create a summary of progress and challenges. They can review the summary components, create action steps with goals to address the challenges, and determine a timeline for completion. These tools guide and move the practice forward, providing an individualized plan for a coach's own growth.

Evaluating Coaches

Teacher evaluation is common practice today, but there are no "off the shelf" rubrics for evaluating instructional coaches. Like all other school professionals, instructional coaches should be evaluated. The quality of their work needs to be examined. The challenge is to find a strategy appropriate to the unique role that coaches perform. Given the responsibilities that typically fall to a coach, few traditional performance metrics are available. For instance, coaches do not spend their time with students, so value-added measures cannot be applied. And given that coaches have confidential relationships with teachers, they do not report about their work in a typical supervisor-employee fashion. That said, there are several approaches to principal evaluations of coaches that make sense to us and a number of ways to gather documentation essential to the evaluation process. Here are some suggestions:

- *Start with the job description.* Like any position in an organization, the first question should be this: Is the coach doing the things that have been agreed upon—the things the coach has been asked to do?
- *Consider surveying teachers (anonymously)* to learn what services their coach provided and how well those services met the needs.
- *Consider what has been learned during regular meetings* school leaders have with coaches. Although the coach is not a surrogate for the school leader, the school leadership team knows a lot about the coach's work—from ongoing discussions of professional development needs and administrative observations at professional development events to understanding how the coach has addressed the schoolwide mission and priorities.
- *Observe the observable.* If the coach is engaged in whole-school and small-group professional development, school leaders can examine how the coach

approaches that work and how well it is carried out. If done well, the product of those professional development opportunities should be clear and visible. Further, there are ways to understand coaching in classrooms. While the *B* (*before*) and the *A* (*after*) are conversations that coaches and teachers hold in confidence, school leaders can certainly see the *D* (*during*) in action in classrooms, including circumstances where coaches are modeling new instructional practices for teachers and sharing their expertise in classroom settings. This can provide considerable insight into a coach's skills in working with individual teachers.

Because of confidentiality, school leaders will not know exactly who a coach is working with day-to-day (or what they are working on). In fact, if the coach is doing the job well, the school leader will certainly *not* know exactly what a coach is doing with each teacher. But the strategies just suggested offer tools for school leaders to learn how coaches perform in general terms and what teachers think of the services they receive.

Coaches and Schoolwide Teacher Evaluation

On this point we are clear: coaches should not, in any way, participate in the evaluation of teachers. The reason is quite straightforward. Coaches work with teachers in a confidential manner; they strive to achieve a trusting relationship. If a coach becomes part of the evaluation process, whether intentionally or not, the relationship with teachers will change.

In education, many teachers have been burned by the "gotcha" factor—an administrator walking into a classroom without any prior communication, "observing" a lesson or snapshot in time, and then sending a checklist of what was or was not done in the classroom without suggestions for specific ways to improve. Instructional coaching can change that paradigm. Coaches work with teachers and their administrators so that a mutually agreed-upon vision of schoolwide improvement is shared by all. They work with administrators to help plan strategic ways to address student needs as a schoolwide endeavor, not to target individual teachers who may be experiencing some classroom challenges.

Coaches work hard to build highly personalized networks. They should not share what they see or discuss with administrators—even the positive things they experience with the individuals they coach. To maintain the bond, coaches cannot be seen as part of the administrative evaluation team without risking their ability to work with teachers around difficult matters of teaching and learning. Coaches are there to support teachers. If coaches begin to look and act like supervisors, the quality and content of their work will be compromised.

Even if administration is aware of the importance of confidentiality and trust in the teacher-coach relationship, a coach may face a lot of pressure to help the principal with evaluations. How does a coach respectfully decline requests to participate in these conversations? Here are some suggestions:

- If asked by the principal to collect evidence of a particular teacher's practice, the coach should remind the principal that the teacher herself has been collecting evidence of performance to share with the administrator.
- If the principal asks the coach specific questions about a teacher's practice, the coach should remind the principal about their partnership agreement, confidentiality, and the fact that the coach's work is nonevaluative. Coaches do not look at a teacher's practice with an evaluative eye.
- Coaches should help teachers they work with understand that administrators want to know and have the right to know what is happening in classrooms. They can suggest that administrators visit classrooms both informally and formally (observations) and watch the everyday elements of practice.
- Coaches must be comfortable and confident enough to remind principals that coaching is to support teachers, collectively solve problems, and think critically about how students learn. They need to remind principals that teachers will try innovative ways to teach if they are given the time to collaborate, talk about practice, rehearse with a nonevaluative partner (the coach), and reflect with that partner. This can only be accomplished if the environment is conducive to risk taking without the fear of being "graded."

One of our colleagues, Coach Michaelson, faced the issue of coaching and teacher evaluation. Here is how she handled it.

....

Declining a Role in the Teacher Evaluation Process

Coach Michaelson has worked with most teachers in each of the departments in the school. She has been developing relationships and strong partnerships for the last three years and is happy with the support and acceptance she has received from the staff. Although the first few months were tricky, she has repeatedly met with the faculty to discuss her role and how she and the teachers can work together.

When the teacher effectiveness framework (TEF, an individual state's teacher evaluation tool) was introduced in the school, the principal asked that the coach be part of the process. The principal knew that the coach worked with teachers to develop goals and collected evidence about improved practice and thought that it was a good idea to include her in this kind of evaluative conversation. The coach was very clear: teachers could choose to share the goals and evidence from the teacher-administrator conversations but that came from the teachers, not the coach's firsthand involvement. She could not be part of an evaluative conversation but would be a willing participant when the teacher came to share what transpired in the conversation with the administrator.

The coach explained to the administrative team that being part of the evaluation process would undermine the coaching interactions and breach confidentiality necessary to sustain trusting relationships. The coach should not be present when an administrator discussed the specific details of a teacher's evaluation. Things could be said that the coach should not hear. That conversation was between teacher and administrator. The teacher was encouraged to privately discuss the evaluation with the coach so that the two of them could plan how to address the areas of needed support.

After the coach explained why she couldn't be part of the evaluation, the administrator supported the coach by honoring that nonevaluative practice and not compromising the strong relationships that she had formed with her teaching colleagues. It was a lesson for everyone: confidentiality is always between the two involved in the actual dialogue.

....

Coaching is confidential, reflective, and nonjudgmental; evaluation is an assessment of the work with a deliberate value placed upon performance. In coaching, the involved partners work together to discuss ways to improve practice and make it better. There is no "final" statement of quality attributed to one action, but, rather, consistent and regular conversations to make continuous improvements. We are quite certain that involving coaches in the teacher evaluation process would make it difficult for coaches to perform their roles effectively.

Summing Up

A coaching practice moves along a continuum of support. Coaches need to continually build awareness of how instructional coaching helps the school community achieve its goals and simultaneously revisit their own goals to ensure they are moving practice forward. But each coaching interaction is personal, intentional, and specific to the individual's needs. So, although some coaching interactions are community oriented, others are deliberately one-on-one; both are designed to help teachers reach their fullest potential and give choice and voice to the individual. This outcome happens when trusting relationships are established, confidentiality is honored, and improving practice is the goal. All staff members are members in a community of learning and practice, investing in the advanced learning of every participant in that school, including administrators who provide ongoing support. Coaches can use the Levels of Intensity and related assessment tools to organize their work and self-assess their progress.

10

Mentors and School Leaders: Supporting Coaches for the Long Run

The growth and development of people is the highest calling of leadership.

—Harvey Firestone

Effective instructional coaches understand that learning is ongoing, situational, intentional, and social. Like the educators with whom they work, coaches should not be left to sink or swim on their own. Given that a coach's work continually evolves to meet changing needs, coaches must have ongoing opportunities to enhance their own skills. Similar to the coach's partnerships with teachers, coaches themselves need experienced, competent partners to help build their skills, ask reflective questions, offer feedback, and suggest ways to improve performance. In this chapter, we consider different ways of supporting instructional coaches: on-site support by school leaders, mentoring, and ongoing professional development, including building networks to reinforce common approaches to coaching and providing a setting for collaborative reflection.

School Leaders and Support for Coaches

Principals and school leaders hold the keys to the kingdom. With their active support, an instructional coach can succeed in gaining access to and generating interest among teachers to help them improve student outcomes. Without that support, a coach may flounder. As noted earlier, principals and school leaders work together with coaches to set the school coaching agenda. Besides promoting the "idea" of instructional coaching and working closely with the coach to establish the parameters of the role, principals and school leaders can help the coach by doing the following:

- *Sharing the vision for coaching with staff that the principal and coach have articulated, and reinforcing the message with staff and parents that this vision is important to achieving the school's mission.* Everyone needs to be on the same page when introducing a new concept to the school community. Inconsistency and misunderstanding will force people to take sides and become competitive, promote hearsay, and damage efforts to collaborate.
- *Respecting that the coach's role is confidential and not part of the teachers' evaluation plan.* Neither coaches nor administrators want teachers to question the support they receive. The administrator and the coach must stand side-by-side and inform the staff that the principal will not ask coaches to be evaluative, nor will the coaches make evaluative comments about teachers to the administrators. No one's trust will be compromised.
- *Accommodating and acknowledging the coach's schedule by not asking the coach to do things that are out of scope, as though the coach is just an available extra body.* Coaches plan their schedules around the BDA cycle of consultation. That means time must be allotted for the coach to prepare for one-on-one conferences and mini professional learning sessions as well as the small-group, coach-led activities. When a coach spends time exploring available resources aligned to instruction and scheduling appointments to discuss those resources, that is time well spent. Asking the coach to forego that planning trivializes the importance and purpose of professional learning, which is the antithesis of implementing an effective instructional coaching model.
- *Giving the coach time to speak and share ideas at meetings.* Coaches should be part of the school leadership team and recognized as someone with skill and a voice to be heard and respected. The school leadership must view coaches as teacher leaders and continuously build awareness and validate the purposes for this job-embedded teacher professional development model. School leaders must publicly share how instructional coaching helps achieve the school-wide goals for improvement.
- *Having the coach lead schoolwide and small-group professional development.* Let the coach organize, promote, and, as appropriate, facilitate these activities. Coaches are tasked with the responsibility of identifying the kinds of professional development needed and then transforming those sessions into professional learning through follow-up and persistent support.

School leadership that recognizes the coach in this fashion will make a real impact on the teaching staff. The coach's role will be clear, and coaches' contributions will be acknowledged, supporting the philosophy that everyone is a learner and that learning is important for the success of the school. The bottom line is this: *The principal and leadership team can show the staff that the instructional coach is always looking for ways to build capacity and enhance teachers' strengths.*

Although principals come and go, if coaches can lay a solid foundation, their mission will be respected, regardless of the current leadership. As big players in the process that helps to change the climate and culture of the school, they become a driving force for sustainable professional development.

Mentors—The Coach's Coach

Mentors are a key component in the educator-centered instructional coaching model. A coach's mentor provides a layer of support that mirrors what coaches offer teachers. Mentors are experienced educators who are well informed about subject matter content, pedagogy, professional development, and the alignment of curriculum to standards. They keep up with trends in education, understand assessment and data analysis and school improvement planning. In other words, the mentor is a well-rounded, veteran educator, a proven performer.

> The other mentors are a huge resource for me. We recommend books to each other, share presentations and materials, and if I'm having a problem I can call a fellow mentor for advice. I couldn't do my work without them. They are a huge part of my professional growth.
>
> —Amy Walker, Mentor

Mentors create professional learning communities for instructional coaches and meet with coaches regularly to help them build their skills and capacity. They, too, follow the BDA cycle of consultation and provide one-on-one and small-group support to coaches and advocate for instructional coaching. They understand the link between research and practice, and they help coaches build trust with teachers and administrators. The relationship between mentor and coach is confidential. Mentors are not supervisors or peers. They help coaches negotiate the partnership between the coach and the administrator, reinforcing the coach's role as nonevaluative; they are not there to report on the coaches' progress with teachers. They support teachers from a distance, and sometimes it is challenging to remember that mentors help coaches help teachers; mentors do not provide direct support to teachers. (If they did, they would be coaches, not mentors!) In effect, the mentor provides coaches with ongoing professional development—tailored to the particular needs of each coach, modeling the differentiated support process that coaches provide to teachers.

Mentors are chosen for their expertise in working collaboratively with others and building trust. This is why they are good advocates for instructional coaching at the district level. They are change agents who understand schools and how coaching fits into the broader context of school improvement.

The coach in a district we worked with struggled in the new school year as he tried to reaffirm his role to the district administration. He was appointed during the school year and with his mentor's support was able to build awareness about his position with the staff before the year ended. Unfortunately, both the superintendent and the curriculum director were reassigned and new administrators were appointed at the opening of school. Although their predecessors were champions of instructional coaching, neither of these newly appointed district administrators were knowledgeable about instructional coaching; their interests were in improving student test scores and parental concerns rather than schoolwide innovations that improved teaching.

Not knowing how to approach the district administrators without jeopardizing the instructional coaching commitment, the coach went to his mentor for advice. Together, they planned the steps that would help bridge the gap between what the district administrators knew and the school's expectations for bolstering teaching and learning and decided on what research to share with them. Here are the steps they planned:

1. Arrange a meeting at the school for the district administrators, school-based administrators, the mentor, and the coach to discuss schoolwide needs and interests.
2. Convene a small group of teachers to talk about why they believed instructional coaching could improve teaching and learning.
3. Share the schoolwide improvement plan, schoolwide data, research about instructional coaching, and goals for improvement, and demonstrate how instructional coaching will help achieve those goals.
4. Invite the administrators to share their expectations for school transformation.
5. Develop an action plan that addresses the needs and supports ongoing professional learning for all.
6. Schedule quarterly meetings to review action plan items and make adjustments to the plans.

The mentor was instrumental in building the coach's confidence and helping plan the steps that would begin to build the administrators' understanding of instructional coaching. The mentor was an active participant in the conversation as well, validating what the coach said and sharing research about instructional coaching to assuage any of the district administrators' doubts. In the end, they were successful in getting the new administrators' buy-in and compromising on a plan to meet schoolwide goals that worked for everyone.

Competencies for Mentoring

Although mentoring and coaching are similar, successful instructional mentoring requires some different competencies. Coaches work directly with teachers to help them change practice; mentors work directly with coaches to help them recognize their own areas of strength and need as well as those of the teachers they coach. Mentors provide feedback to the coaches and work to collectively problem-solve around individual and community issues with the ultimate goal of moving practice forward. Mentors are accomplished practitioners who practice from a distance. They help coaches acknowledge their own preferences, understand how those preferences influence their coaching interactions, and cultivate their practices so that ultimately they can enrich and reinforce authentic practice in the classroom.

To help administrators and mentors understand the scope and required competencies of instructional mentoring, Pennsylvania developed a document to support the role and function of the position. It is one example of a state's guidelines for mentoring qualifications and responsibilities (see Appendix B for the complete document). The Pennsylvania guidelines do the following:

- Describe in detail the role of the coach mentor
- Emphasize the nonsupervisory/nonevaluative nature of the role
- List the qualifications for the role, including a valid teaching certificate, five years' teaching experience, experience in planning and facilitating professional learning opportunities, and other requirements
- Outline the responsibilities of the role, including site visits, one-on-one support to coaches, collaboration with school leadership, and other activities
- Emphasize the need for continual improvement in practice through professional development for the mentor
- Highlight the importance of relationships in the mentoring role
- Specify the supervisors to whom the mentor reports

Mentors work with administrators to reinforce the coaching role; they advocate for instructional coaching at the district and intermediate unit (educational service agency) levels. Mentors continually research how teachers and their students learn and put that research into practice. They work with coaches to enhance the coaches' toolkit with a variety of tools to address a multitude of issues. And very often, mentors help coaches navigate their new relationships with each other. The following account provides an example of the latter situation.

Reconciling Differences and Enhancing Practice

The coaching office in one school where we worked was very small, with two desks side-by-side. The mentor and coaches tried their best to configure the space but knew it would be a challenge. Ms. Nguyen had a very quiet, serious approach to the coaching role, spending more time getting to know the teachers before jumping into the coaching responsibilities. Mr. Everett was more jovial and had a "no problem" type of response to helping his teaching colleagues. He was more inclined to tell rather than listen and to give his opinion rather than help his teaching colleagues come to their own conclusions. His one-on-one conversations dwindled and became very sporadic. He was happy to adopt a "they'll come when they have a question" approach rather than to seek out his colleagues and engage in professional conversations. Ms. Nguyen, on the other hand, continued to schedule regular meetings with her colleagues, following the BDA cycle of consultation.

Although coaching is not a cookie-cutter practice with programmed responses, there are certain behaviors that are repeated with each person who is coached. For instance, every coaching interaction should begin with "teacher talk," not "coach talk"—with the teacher sharing what she thinks is important and how the coach can help, not with the coach telling the teacher what she needs to do in class. In the case of Ms. Nguyen and Mr. Everett, the mentor regularly reminded both coaches to listen more than they spoke.

Once the two coaches established relationships with their teachers, they created a schedule for office conferences. After talking with their mentor, they decided which periods per day would be devoted to their coaching cohorts' one-on-one office conversations and which periods would be dedicated to small-group mini professional development sessions. They soon learned that one-on-one conversations also occurred when teachers came to the office unannounced.

In the beginning, the schedules worked effectively; each coach had dedicated time for the one-on-one *before* and *after* conversations. However, that schedule began to deteriorate as more and more teachers wanted to engage in the planning, or *before*, sessions with Ms. Nguyen. Mr. Everett began to feel uncomfortable because he was not engaging in as many one-on-one conversations. He began staying in the office longer when Ms. Nguyen was conferencing with her teachers. Eventually it became obvious that he was listening, and he slowly started to intervene with his opinions. Ms. Nguyen tried to politely remind Mr. Everett that there were specific "office conference hours" and that they should both be sensitive to the confidential nature of those conversations and adhere to the schedule. He agreed in theory but not in practice. He continued to stick around the office and ultimately made no attempt to leave.

Not wanting to go to the administration, Ms. Nguyen approached the mentor and asked for help. She knew that her mentor was skilled in problem solving, interpersonal relationships, and what she needed most, diplomacy, in communicating with her office mate.

The mentor listened to Ms. Nguyen explain the situation and suggested that they all meet together to establish norms, something they had not done before. The mentor wanted to get to the root cause of why Mr. Everett was ignoring the agreed-upon conditions for office conferencing time and suspected that he didn't know how to generate more one-on-one conversations and wanted to learn from Ms. Nguyen. The mentor presumed positive intentions and hoped Ms. Nguyen could adopt that thinking as well.

Developing norms was a nonthreatening, noninvasive starting point. It not only gave both coaches an opportunity to share what was important to them but also revealed different views on coaching, which created a teachable moment for the mentor to intercede and help the coaches learn from each other.

Changes were slow but steady, and within the year, the two coaches made great progress in understanding how their viewpoints and learning affected their coaching styles. They learned that the office hours were not the issue; the real issue was that Mr. Everett was not as comfortable as Ms. Nguyen was with convening one-on-one conversations. He learned from her actions how to change that paradigm. The mentor demonstrated her agility in determining root causes and was able to transform their thinking and practice over time. Without the mentor, Ms. Nguyen would have had no alternative but to go to the administration for help, which would have undermined the essence of instructional coaching—maintaining confidentiality to support all kinds of learning.

The mentor's work parallels the coach's work. The BDA cycle of consultation and feedback is fundamental to the way mentors work with coaches, just as it is for coaches and teachers. The process is similar whether the mentor is meeting with coaches one-on-one or in a group:

- *Before* meeting with coaches, mentors collect school and district demographic information and review school improvement plans so they can help coaches plan how they will work with teachers to improve student achievement. Using this data, mentors meet with coaches to co-create goals, help determine strategies, and identify materials and resources coaches can use with their teachers.
- *During* visits with the coaches, mentors have two goals: (1) to work with coaches to identify specific instructional approaches that meet the teachers' needs and that emphasize the consistency of language and practice across all content areas; and (2) to collect data to provide feedback to coaches about how they are working with teachers using the data they co-constructed in their *before* consultation. Mentors are silent partners while coaches work one-on-one with teachers.
- *After* the visit, mentors meet one-on-one with each coach to debrief and offer feedback, focusing on the coach's next steps to help the teachers with whom they are working improve student learning. This is a nonevaluative process that encourages coaches to try innovative ways to engage teachers in a risk-free environment. Mentors model the process with coaches that coaches are expected to model with teachers.

But even before this cycle of consultation, mentors should invest time into getting to know their coaches. They have to build a level of trust and interest in working together. Figure 10.1 serves as a quick guide that can help mentors get to know the coaches with whom they work; and the following recollection demonstrates the importance of establishing a solid working relationship.

Ellen's Experience with Her Mentor

When I think back to one of my earliest experiences working with a mentor, I remember that the mentor did not focus on the question I asked. Instead, she started talking about teaching in general and asked me what I wanted to accomplish when working with teachers. I was surprised, because I had a specific question and wanted to focus on that, especially since we were talking during the time I needed to research some topics for a teacher team with whom I was working.

Figure 10.1 Getting to Know You: Questions for Mentors to Ask Coaches

Coaching Experience
- How long have you been an instructional coach? Have you always coached at this grade level?
- Why did you choose to become an instructional coach?
- What, to you, is the best thing about being an instructional coach?
- What do you think is the most difficult thing about being an instructional coach?

Coaching Style
- How would you describe your current coaching style? What are your strengths? In what areas would you like to improve?
- Do you have a set of guidelines? If so, what are those guidelines?
- How do you handle teachers who do not want to be coached?
- When working with a teacher, what strategies have you found to be most effective for you? What strategies have you found to be ineffective?

Past Consultation Experiences
- What has been your past experience with coaching or mentoring? What did you find helpful?
- Ideally, what would you like to have happen when consulting with another professional?
- How often do you receive feedback on your coaching? How often do you give feedback?
- What are some of the things you like or dislike about giving and receiving feedback?
- If given a choice between receiving face-to-face feedback and a printout or an e-mail summary of data collected on your coaching, which do you think you would prefer? Why? How do you give feedback?

Specific Areas of Support
- What are some of the challenges in coaching you see?
- Do you have challenging teachers who are not currently being coached and would most likely benefit from more individualized support? How many? How might you approach these teachers?

Coaching Goals
- What are your coaching goals for this year?
- Are you interested in facilitating some instructional learning visits where a team of teachers take turns and visit each other's classrooms? This is a coach-led collaborative school improvement process using study group and planning group activities following the BDA cycle of learning.
- Would you be interested in having your peers shadow you on a coaching cycle? This would have to be prescheduled and approved by the teacher.

The mentor could sense that I was anxious about our conversation even though I was the one who had approached her. She continued our conversation by asking about my experiences being coached and what I did or didn't like about the experiences, followed by what I had learned through those experiences.

I have to admit, I was not expecting this kind of opening dialogue. I thought we would get right into the question I had about a particular issue.

Of course, I soon realized that the mentor was trying to get acquainted with me and my style of coaching, which impacted my style of coaching with the teachers. What really surprised me was when she asked, "How would you like to work with me?" She was really giving me a voice and choice about our mentoring-coaching interactions.

We actually met two more times before the conversation about my practice with the teachers emerged. Interestingly, I started asking the teachers some of the very same questions my mentor asked me. It reminded me of my interviews for teaching, when the committee asked me, "What is your philosophy of teaching and learning?" I didn't know then what I know now—an individual's values and preferences certainly sway one's actions!

Guiding Questions for Mentoring

Any interaction between and among mentors, coaches, teachers, and administrators requires thoughtful planning. Once mentors get to know their coaches and get a sense of their coaches' needs, it is time to take it to the next level, which, as noted earlier, often includes advocating for instructional coaching and digging into the BDA cycle with the coach. Frequently, mentors become the voice for instructional coaching with school administrators, cultivating positive relationships that might otherwise challenge the coach. Here are some questions the mentor might reflect on in preparation (the mentor's "before the *before*" planning) for meeting with the coach and the subsequent conference scheduled with the principal:

- What does the principal know about instructional coaching?
- Has the principal ever coached or been coached?
- Does the principal think coaching is a random strategy or one that requires planning and deliberate scheduling?
- How does the principal think coaching "works"?
- Did the principal give the staff an opportunity to talk about coaching as a way to help achieve their schoolwide improvement goals before adopting a coaching model?

Mentors also benefit from some guiding questions to drive conversations with coaches and administrators throughout their BDA cycle:

Before
- What is your understanding of instructional coaching?

- What are the district's goals for schoolwide improvement and how do you envision coaching will help your school achieve those goals?
- How was your coaching role shared with the staff? What do you think your colleagues understand about instructional coaching?
- What do you think are the intended outcomes of coaching and working with your colleagues?
- How much time would you like to spend working with your colleagues? What are some of the things you noticed as a _____ [reading specialist, classroom teacher, or other role] that can help you in your coaching role?
- When do you have regularly scheduled meetings with the principal? How are the agendas constructed?
- How do you think we should approach the staff? What are some of the things we should focus on when building awareness with the staff?
- What would you like my role to be in this situation? What data, if any, would you like me to collect?

During

The mentor collects data when the coach meets with the principal, refers to the co-constructed agenda items, shares some research about instructional coaching with the principal, and is a partner throughout the meeting. At the meeting, the mentor might ask the principal the following questions:

- What are some of the ways you [the principal] envision the coach working with the staff?
- How can we help the staff members to understand the differences between intervention and support?
- What would you like the coach to focus on when working with staff members?

After

These are questions for the coach and the mentor to discuss:

- What do you think the principal understands about instructional coaching as a result of the meeting?
- What are some of the ways you plan to approach the staff and renegotiate your role as a coach as a result of the meeting?
- How can you reinforce the understanding of your coaching role with your colleagues?
- How will you determine your schedule for meeting with teachers now that you know the principal's expectations for coaching?

- What, if anything, got in the way of the principal understanding your coaching role?
- What are your next steps in helping the staff understand instructional coaching and the differences between coaching and intervention?

Levels of Intensity for Mentoring

Just as there are Levels of Intensity for coaches (see Figures 9.1 and 9.2 in Chapter 9), there are similar Levels of Intensity for mentors (Figures 10.2 and 10.3). As with coaching, these levels are dynamic. A mentor may be in more-intense practice with some coaches than with others, it may take a longer or shorter period of time to develop a deeper practice with some coaches than with others, and the mentor may be more ready to move along the continuum in some areas of practice than in others. As noted, mentors follow the same BDA cycle of consultation to engage with the coaches around the coaching framework. The Levels of Intensity help mentors assess where they are in the mentoring practice and how they can help coaches move from one level to another. Keep in mind, the Levels of Intensity are contextual. They vary according to a variety of factors: coaching experience, staff experience, length of schoolwide coaching implementation, school receptivity, and so on.

In many ways, the levels for mentors parallel those for coaches as described in Chapter 9, but the model does have its own unique features. As with coaching, the levels of mentoring intensity represent increasingly deeper practice. Every element

Figure 10.2 Examples of Levels of Intensity for Instructional Mentors

> **Level 1: Basic; helps to develop relationships with coaches**
> - Helping coaches build awareness of the BDA cycle of coaching and the four core elements
> - Helping coaches unpack the Common Core State Standards, websites, and the various statewide initiatives
> - Providing one-on-one and small-group support to coaches (identifying issues or needs, setting goals, problem solving)
> - Helping coaches understand one-on-one coaching, small-group support, and our literacy framework
> - Assisting coaches in recruiting districts, schools, teachers, and other school leaders for implementing an instructional coaching model
> - Developing and providing materials for and with coaches (acting as a resource provider)
> - Participating in professional development activities with coaches at the school, district, and intermediate unit levels, and other statewide meetings and conferences
> - Planning, reviewing, and establishing the process for study groups, book studies, and effective PLCs
> - Helping coaches understand various kinds of formative and summative data, what data are necessary, and how to use the collected data

Level 2: More formal, somewhat more intense; mentor helps the coach focus on areas of need and how to support adult learners

- Reinforcing the BDA cycle of coaching and the four core elements through modeling and watching as coaches work with teachers
- Co-planning with coaches to use a variety of formative assessment strategies with staff
- Supporting coaches in the educator-effectiveness process as they help teachers establish goals for growth and develop their own goals
- Helping coaches identify teacher needs in planning units of study
- Helping coaches plan agendas for team meetings
- Helping coaches understand data reports and what the data say about instruction
- Assessing the strengths of the instructional coach, providing resources to support the coach's skill set, and providing professional learning opportunities to address the coach's needs
- Helping coaches model effective strategies for increasing student engagement and improving student achievement
- Convening coaches' meetings and networking opportunities
- Supporting coaches in nonevaluative consultation and reflective practices
- Co-planning follow-up professional development after conferences and other professional development sessions

Level 3: Formal, more intense; deepening the conversations around instructional coaching, increasing student engagement, improving student achievement, and changing practices

- Deepening the use of the BDA cycle and the four core elements
- Helping coaches implement the *after* phase of the BDA cycle regularly
- Facilitating professional learning around evidence-based literacy strategies
- Modeling coaching techniques via scenarios and other professional learning opportunities
- Co-planning and co-facilitating professional learning opportunities
- Visiting classrooms with coaches and providing feedback to coaches
- Analyzing videotape lessons of teachers with coaches, where applicable
- Submitting proposals for presentations to state and national conferences
- Facilitating cross-district visitations and schoolwide instructional learning visits
- Advocating nonevaluative and reflective practices
- Supporting the educator-effectiveness process and the coach's role in helping teachers implement effective instructional practices across all content areas

Source: From "Promoting Effective Literacy Instruction: The Challenge for Literacy Coaches," by R. M. Bean, Spring 2004, *The California Reader, 37*(3), pp. 58–63. Copyright 2004 by The California Reading Association. Adapted with permission.

in each level requires recognition of an individual coach's strengths and calculated tailoring of mentoring objectives to meet individual needs. That being said, the mentor's skill set and knowledge base are critical for helping coaches grow in their practice through the differentiated support offered to coaches in small groups and one-on-one interactions. Using these tables helps keep the mentors focused on their deliberate and intentional work with the coaches.

One mentor we have worked with, Diane Hubona, pays particular attention to these Levels of Intensity, mixing them up according to the needs of the instructional coaches. At the first level, she is a resource provider, and, as she observes, "some veteran coaches only need that." At the second level, she might model a lesson for a coach or co-teach with the teacher. Hubona's goal at the third level is for the coaches to start solving problems themselves and to seek collaboration with other coaches. The levels are decided on a needs-only basis. What the coaches need determines the support they receive.

Hubona agrees that communication skills are especially important to mentors, primarily because they must retain a good relationship with their instructional coaches over the long haul. She estimates that it takes about three years for an instructional coach to become comfortable in the role and an integral part of the job-embedded professional development model. Also, she says, mentors need strong organizational skills and the ability to develop great questioning techniques. "The point is to guide coaches, not direct them," she says.

Hubona sometimes finds herself becoming an advocate for instructional coaching with school administrations. She provides superintendents with descriptions of instructional coaching, and when one district wanted to cut the coaching position, she worked with the coach to advocate for instructional coaching with appropriate schoolwide data to show how instructional coaching affected students, teachers, and classrooms. So far, she says, "we haven't lost a position even when other internal changes were made."

This kind of personalized support is essential to meet the needs of the individual, but there are creative ways of making it happen. For example, coaches blend their approach so that they provide both face-to-face and virtual support to the teachers with whom they work, but they are typically in the buildings every day with their teaching colleagues. Mentors, however, more often work to enhance coaches' skills from a distance because their coaches work across many schools and districts. The following example, based on the experience of a mentor with whom we worked, illustrates how mentors and their coaches can blend the support they give to their teaching colleagues.

Communicating in Various Ways

Upon noticing that several coaches wanted to ask her questions via e-mail, Ms. Findlay decided to create a survey asking her coaches how they wanted her to communicate with them, when they were most likely to be available, and how often she should expect responses from them electronically. Because she was not present every day in any coach's school, she knew that a good deal of communication would have to be electronic and wondered how much she should rely on e-mail for collective problem solving or collaborative planning. She recognized that electronic communication had limits. For instance, most people only read short e-mails. If she had a list of questions where one question led to a longer series of questions, the coach would not have the time or interest in answering them all. That she would need to do in person. She wanted to ensure that ongoing discussions yielded positive changes in practice and needed to see the person to determine if her communication was clear and easy to understand. She wanted to ensure that her conversations were targeted and specific, always right to the point, and felt that was easier to accomplish in person than in an e-mail. She also didn't want any tone to be misconstrued and wanted to ensure that emphasis on either language or idea was taken as intended.

The coaches were thrilled to know that this mentor was willing to communicate virtually and suggested that she establish two venues for communication: (1) "Ask the mentor" virtual sessions so they could ask specific questions about things they wanted to know more about and (2) post virtual office hours so they could "visit" her during the scheduled hours and discuss plans about instruction or instructional practices. They thought their *before* sessions could be electronic, followed by a more in-depth face-to-face conversation, deepening their understanding of how their goals could be achieved. They also thought that offering some web-based alternatives for collaboration would be an effective way to connect the team of coaches when face-to-face collaboration was not possible. The mentor and the coaches collaborated on finding the balance they needed to blend the virtual with the face-to-face with two nonnegotiable caveats: (1) at the time of the first electronic communication, the mentor set a date with the coaches for the face-to-face meeting; and (2) both the *during* visit and the *after* debriefing sessions could not be facilitated electronically. The coaches clearly understood that the depth of their conversation could not be accomplished by communicating only electronically.

Once the preliminary electronic communication took place, Ms. Findlay followed up with the face-to-face support. The coaches appreciated Ms. Findlay's flexibility in understanding that her mentoring "in real time" could actually be accomplished electronically to a certain extent and that nothing really takes the place of a face-to-face visit. As one coach remarked,

Figure 10.3 Summary of Levels of Intensity for Mentors

Intensity Area	Level 1 Informal; helps to develop relationships	Level 2 More formal, somewhat more intense; begins to look at areas of need or focus	Level 3 Formal, more intense; moves interactions from general to specific
Coaches' Networking Meetings	Planning and facilitating coaches' networking meetings	Modeling facilitation of effective professional learning opportunities for adult learners through monthly coaches' networking meetings	Providing feedback to coaches on content, process, and format of networking meetings
BDA and the Four Core Elements	Building coaches' and administrators' awareness of adult learning, the BDA cycle of coaching, one-on-one and small-group support, and the four core elements	Reinforcing the BDA cycle of coaching and the four core elements through modeling and watching as coaches work with teachers	Deepening the BDA cycle and the four core elements through the effective use of clarifying and probing questions; listening for limiting beliefs; facilitating the reframing process; developing self-awareness of strengths and challenges
Professional Learning Opportunities	Building coaches' and administrators' awareness of available resources (e.g., resource guide, websites, conferences)	Co-planning/co-facilitating effective professional learning opportunities with coaches for teachers, including follow-up from conferences and other PD	Supporting coaches in finding and developing effective and appropriate materials to support instruction and to enhance the coach's own skill set
Evidence-Based Literacy	Modeling effective coaching practices, including professional development activities, evidence-based literacy practices, nonevaluative and reflective practices	Co-planning and co-facilitating with coaches using various evidence-based literacy practices, nonevaluative and reflective practices with staff	Observing and providing feedback to coaches on their support and use of evidence-based literacy practices, nonevaluative and reflective practices

Intensity Area	Level 1 Informal; helps to develop relationships	Level 2 More formal, somewhat more intense; begins to look at areas of need or focus	Level 3 Formal, more intense; moves interactions from general to specific
Needs Assessment and Continuous Improvement	Creating a schoolwide needs assessment or other strategies to identify needs	Co-developing an action plan for continuous improvement designed to meet schoolwide and districtwide goals	Engaging coaches in conversations about the action plan and how schoolwide needs are being met as part of a continuous improvement process
Improvement of Classroom Practices	Developing and providing materials for coaches to support improved classroom instruction	Modeling the use of evidence-based literacy and other classroom practices that are applicable to all content areas	Providing opportunities for reflective feedback and collective problem solving around using literacy strategies and other classroom practices
	Building coach awareness of state standards and current statewide initiatives	Supporting coaches to deepen their understanding of and make connections to state standards, the state's teacher effectiveness process, and the various statewide initiatives	Supporting coaches in facilitating teacher implementation of state standards, the state's teacher effectiveness process, and the various statewide initiatives
	Helping coaches differentiate and identify the purposes of formative, summative, benchmark, and diagnostic assessments	Creating opportunities for coaches to understand the various kinds of formative and summative data and how to analyze and use the collected data	Supporting coaches to look at data systemically and use data to implement instructional or curricular changes

"Sending questions to my doctor about my medications via e-mail is great when I only have one question with one expected answer. Deeper questions getting to the heart of a practice often result in several possibilities that all need to be dissected, distilled, and digested. I can't do that electronically."

Communication either makes you or breaks you! Mentors keep the lines of communication open by creating an environment that is conducive to ongoing conversations that are inviting, nonjudgmental, and nonthreatening. They are skilled colleagues who remove the barriers of communication by keeping coaches and the teachers with whom they work connected in an era where disconnection and disenfranchisement can easily occur. By helping coaches recognize the importance of deliberate conversations around increasing student engagement and building teacher capacity, mentors reinforce the idea that time to collaborate, plan, think, and work together is made, not found in the hallway, parking lot, restrooms, or teachers' lounge. Also, the time, place, and method of communication must be differentiated according to the topic and need.

Professional Development

In addition to administrative support and mentoring, ongoing professional development is the third leg of the coach's support system. Professional development can be self-initiated or it can come from networking or learning communities. The important point is that mentors and coaches, like all other professionals, need ongoing *dedicated* opportunities to grow on the job. Professional development for coaches is built around three main areas: (1) building a solid coaching foundation, (2) supporting classroom instruction, and (3) collaborating with school leaders.

Building a Solid Coaching Foundation

Learning the tools of the trade requires skill building around a host of critical issues in both content and process. Typical areas appropriate for professional development include the following:

- Coaching the adult learner
- Relationship building and negotiating the coaching role
- Differentiated coaching
- Understanding the language of coaching
- Developing coaching action plans
- Gaining access to teachers and classrooms

- Assessing teachers' needs
- Overcoming resistance
- Understanding and applying each element of the educator-centered instructional coaching framework
- Setting goals
- Having difficult conversations
- Collaboration and collective problem-solving techniques
- Learning the art of reflective questioning
- Developing communication, presentation, and facilitation skills

Read, reflect on your own coaching experiences, and work with your mentor network and colleagues to establish an understanding of instructional coaching and mentoring and how they change practice.

Supporting Classroom Instruction

To help teachers improve classroom instruction, coaches need professional development in many areas, including the following:

- Implementing the BDA cycle
- Applying evidence-based literacy practices to support instruction
- Collecting and using data to inform practice and improve instruction
- Initiating book study groups
- Establishing professional learning communities
- Building students' 21st century learning skills
- Applying appropriate web tools and fostering digital literacy
- Designing and modeling effective lessons
- Curriculum mapping
- Sharing effective classroom management techniques

Attending national conferences, collaborating with colleagues, and establishing a regional and statewide coaching network are activities that support ongoing learning for coaches and mentors, who must model the significance of continuous learning in both ritual and philosophy.

Collaborating With School Leaders

Coaches cannot work effectively without the support of school leaders, so typical professional development in this area includes topics such as the following:

- Sharing a vision for school improvement
- Developing a partnership between coaches and school leaders

- Negotiating the coaching role
- Planning effective professional development for school leaders and teachers
- Evaluating coaches

Coaches and mentors need to work with their administrators to create a shared vision of schoolwide improvement and the plan for accomplishing the goals. That vision must be shared with the staff to ensure understanding and intent of implementing an effective instructional coaching model. School leaders must present a united front with the coach and mentor and generate a systems approach to schoolwide change. At the same time, all parties need to understand that although the vision, goals, and delivery system are public, the conversations between and among all staff are not.

Summing Up

Remember, a coach's practice mirrors the mentor's practice, so whatever the mentor models in her relationships with coaches, the coaches "turn around" those strategies and model them for their teachers. Coaches experience strategies firsthand with their mentors, sculpt the practices to meet the needs of their teachers, and then demonstrate these practices in real time with the teachers they coach.

The coach's coach, the mentor, is an integral part of the process, providing a support system, an experienced eye, and a neutral voice on school matters. Mentors are often the liaisons between the coaches and the school leaders, offering alternative viewpoints and asking probing or clarifying questions. In some cases, the mentor may initiate a difficult conversation best introduced by an outside source. Every level of the school community should have support—the students supported by the teachers, the teachers supported by the coach, the coach supported by the mentor, and the administrators supported by the coach and the mentor. This is a tiered approach that directs the support at each level of commitment.

11

Final Thoughts

You cannot teach today the same way you did yesterday to prepare students for tomorrow.

—John Dewey

Educator-centered instructional coaching offers an opportunity for schools to adopt a different kind of professional development—to throw out the traditional playbook and rethink how to best help teachers do their work. Despite considerable research on the failure of most professional development to change practice, schools continue to offer more of the same. Why is this so? Ingrained habits? A lack of outside funding? No interest in finding out what works? Or the common misconception that just giving teachers information somehow guarantees a transfer of professional learning, when in fact teachers need help in understanding how to use the information they get from professional development? Unfortunately, schools often just continue doing what they have always done because they do not understand that school transformation without continual support will not succeed.

We urge policymakers and school and district administrators to take stock. What is the range of professional development activities offered? What needs are these activities expected to meet? Do the teacher participants feel as though these activities are responsive to their needs? What do teachers want to see in terms of support?

Taking Steps in a New Direction

Accepting the notion that ongoing personalized and comprehensive professional development is one of the most important, sustainable ways in which teachers can improve their practice, perhaps it is time to reexamine what we do and how we do it. In that spirit, educator-centered instructional coaching was designed as a job-embedded teacher professional development framework and tested in the field, yielding positive results. But be advised: as we have noted throughout this book, instituting an instructional coaching initiative requires considerable commitment and effort. It is not a quick fix. We suggest the following steps to get started.

Assess the Need and the Cost

Assess the professional development needs of the district or school. Explore the relationship between current professional development commitments and the needs articulated by teachers and school leaders. Identify the commonalities and the differences. Consider how well the needs are being served. Identify any gaps as opportunities. Then assess cost. How much is spent supporting the current professional development opportunities and what could be done if some of these funds were redirected? Brainstorm some ways to identify funding opportunities. (See Chapter 4 for more on this.)

Consider the costs in terms of the potential for benefits. Instructional coaching is not a cost-free enterprise, but it may be cost-neutral. Just like every other kind of professional development, an instructional coach can be a line item in a school or district budget (even if funded through a special program like Title I or a school improvement grant). Examine the costs and outcomes of traditional approaches to professional development against the costs and outcomes of educator-centered instructional coaching. From all we have learned, we maintain that the long-term impact of instructional coaching will be stronger and ensure more robust outcomes for students and teachers than isolated, unconnected, drop-in professional development. In their analysis of current professional development, education leaders might envision that the ideal professional support for teachers would provide individualized guidance for new teachers, help all teachers move to higher levels of competence, refresh and enrich everyone's knowledge base, and give opportunities for excellent teachers to take leadership roles without moving away from the classroom environment. Specific support around a new program or mandate would still be needed, but these would be part of a schoolwide professional learning community, not apart from it. Frankly, such a vision flows right into instructional coaching—done to scale.

Test and Calibrate the Framework

The devil is in the details—specifically, three details essential to successful implementation of educator-centered instructional coaching: fidelity, ubiquity, and dosage.

- *Fidelity*. Stick closely to the framework. Poor replication may result in a poor product.
- *Ubiquity*. Get everyone involved. It is not enough to "try" educator-centered instructional coaching with a few teachers just to see how it "feels." Every representative group should be part of the conversation. The objective is to involve the entire school community so there is a shared vision. This vision must be revisited regularly to ensure that goals are met.
- *Dosage*. Occasional contact with an instructional coach is not enough. Remember, the objective is to establish a new way of delivering professional development and building capacity and professional learning. There has to be enough coaching to provide everyone with an opportunity to experience the framework in action. Regardless of the number of people involved, they must all have about the same amount of coaching.

Take the Pulse

Carefully assess the progress of coaching, how teachers and school leaders are responding, what differences it is making to teachers in classrooms, and—most important—how differences in instructional practices affect student engagement and achievement. This step can be accomplished in various ways, including ongoing conversations, surveys, benchmarking, and end-of-year progress reports tied to needs assessment. Once on track for continued success, policymakers and practitioners can use what is learned to set the stage for the next step: expanding access to coaching beyond a single school.

The Way Forward

A learning community that adopts our approach to instructional coaching focuses on continuous improvement and is mindful of the needs of everyone in it, recognizing that all are learners, including coaches, mentors, teachers, administrators, and students. It moves the process of improving practice away from evaluations and test scores and toward a collaborative process in which meaningful learning is central. In this important work, educators go beyond standards and directives to focus on the most crucial task of all: making a positive difference for students. The following anecdote, adapted from Taylor Mali (2002, pp. 28–29), captures the essence of this work:

What Do Coaches Make?

The dinner guests were sitting around the table discussing life. One man, a CEO, decided to explain the problem with education. He argued, "What's a kid going to learn from someone who decided his best option in life was to become a teacher?" He reminded the other dinner guests what they say about teachers: "Those who can, do. Those who can't, teach." To stress his point, he said to another guest that he had read about schools now hiring coaches. "What a waste," he remarked. "Teachers go to college; why do they need coaches? You're a coach, Melinda. Be honest. Why do teachers need coaches? That's squandering money. What do you make?"

Melinda, who had a reputation for honesty and frankness replied, "You want to know what I make?"

I make teachers reach their potential more than they ever thought they could.

I make a tough teaching moment feel like the best learning experience ever.

I make learning with colleagues the gold standard.

"You want to know what I make?"

I make teachers wonder.

I make them question.

I make them think outside the box.

I make them reflective.

I make teachers recognize that teaching is a natural wonder of the world . . . they wonder how to make it better for their students.

I make student engagement and learning the centerpiece of teachers' work.

I make teachers feel the value of working together in a world of isolation.

I make teachers see that closed doors do not mean closed minds.

I make teachers feel valued, appreciated, honored, and respected.

I make a difference. What do you make?

Appendix A: Sample Job Description

Job Description for Coaches in Pennsylvania Coaching Initiatives

Role of the Coach

The coach serves as part of their school's leadership team, providing job-embedded and ongoing professional development for teachers, staff, and administration. He/she provides support to the principal in data analysis and professional development decision-making. He/she provides professional development and guidance for teachers to improve their content knowledge and instructional strategies. Overall, the job of the coach is to build the capacity of the school and its teachers to meet the learning needs of all students. The coach's goal is to ensure that school staff acquires the understanding and skills to:

1) enhance instructional practices at the classroom level and
2) raise the level of student achievement.

The effective coach spends the majority of the time working in classrooms with teachers (e.g., modeling, observing, co-teaching). The coach plays a very strong role in the analysis and utilization of student achievement data to impact instructional decision-making. He/she should not, however, be responsible for the administration of assessments, collection of assessment data, or management of data systems. The focus of the coach's work is to help teachers learn to use data for instructional planning that will have a positive impact on student achievement. In that role, the coach helps the teacher learn how to administer and interpret various assessment tools.

The coach may facilitate teacher study groups in which they analyze student work and lesson plans and plan for the enhancement of instructional strategies. The coach's analysis of student work and teaching and learning data will inform what occurs during coaching sessions with individual teachers and in the teacher study groups.

The roles and responsibilities of the coach include:

- Participating in all required coach professional development. The coach is charged with acquiring the knowledge, skills, technology skills, and instructional strategies necessary to effectively impact the instructional practices of the teachers that are coached. He/she must remain knowledgeable about current and past research in the specific content area and other pedagogies relevant to the coaching role.
- Identifying school teaching and learning needs, barriers and weaknesses by analyzing student data, and organizing and implementing problem-solving actions with teachers;
- Facilitating school-based high quality professional development, working with teachers (in teams or individually) to refine their knowledge and skills. Professional development could include, but not be limited to, in-class coaching, observing, modeling of instructional strategies, guiding teachers in looking at student work, developing lesson plans with teachers based on student needs, supporting data analysis, supporting the integration of technology, and co-planning with teachers, and so on;
- Monitoring instructional effectiveness and student progress using tools and strategies gained through professional development;
- Building and maintaining confidential relationships with teachers. The conversations and interactions that the coach has with teachers must always remain confidential so that a high level of trust is created and maintained between the teacher and the coach. Exceptions to this include imminent physical or psychological danger to the students

The coach reports directly to and is held accountable by the school principal or other appropriately certified supervisory personnel. He/she is evaluated annually through the same form as instructional staff (PDE-426, PDE-427, and PDE-428 or locally developed/PDE approved form).

Coach is Non-Supervisory

The role of a coach is separate and apart from the evaluative role of the principal or supervisor of the teacher. The coach advocates for, facilitates, and supports the work of the teacher, but never performs supervision or evaluation. The coach should not confuse providing teachers with consultative feedback requiring professional judgment with supervisory or evaluative responsibilities of the principal. Evaluation, for example, includes completing the teacher evaluation forms PDE-426, PDE-427, and PDE-428. The role of evaluator is the sole responsibility of the principal or supervisor.

Qualifications of the Coach

The effectiveness of any coaching initiative hinges on the selection of a candidate that is highly qualified as a teacher, knowledgeable in content, and skilled in the sophisticated practices of coaching. Districts must select the coach that meets the following criteria:

- Pennsylvania Level II teaching certification in the relevant content area(s);
- Track record or evidence of improving student achievement in their classroom;
- Demonstrated deep knowledge of the relevant content areas;
- Demonstrated knowledge and use of a rich array of instructional approaches, resources, and technologies in the relevant content area(s);
- Demonstrated skills in analyzing and using data for instructional decision-making;
- Interpersonal, problem-solving, and organizational skills required to effectively facilitate coaching and staff development;
- Ability to design and/or broker (individually or in collaboration with others) high quality professional development for teachers/school staff;
- Knowledge of equity issues in current education reform;
- Knowledge and skills to implement a standards-based education system and familiarity with the Pennsylvania Assessment Anchors.

Source: Pennsylvania Department of Education. (n.d.). Retrieved from http://www.education. pa.gov/Documents/Teachers-Administrators/Instructional%20Coaching%20in%20PA/Job%20 Description%20for%20Coaches%20in%20Pennsylvania%20Coaching%20Initiatives.pdf

Appendix B:
Guidelines for the Coach Mentor Position

Role of the Coach Mentor	The Coach Mentor is responsible for planning, facilitating and implementing centralized and school-based professional learning for coaches and administrators. When the Coach Mentor visits the school site, s/he meets with the instructional coach(es) and the school's leadership team, both as a group and individually, to assist in problem-solving and in developing yearly action plans for school reform and improved student achievement (in coordination with NCLB/PDE related School Improvement Plans and Strategic Plans). The Coach Mentor's goal is to ensure that the coaches and administrators have the opportunity to acquire the understanding and skills necessary to implement research-based instructional practices, increase student engagement, build teacher capacity and raise the level of student achievement.
	The Coach Mentor develops a professional learning community for all instructional coaches—those just beginning in the role of instructional coach, as well as those with experience. In this non-supervisory role, the Coach Mentor acts as a critical friend by providing assistance, structure and guidance to instructional coaches in support of the schools' instructional goals and students' achievement goals, when and where needed. Focusing on instructional coaches' strengths, the Coach Mentor collaborates with the instructional coaches in their efforts to help teachers transform classrooms to 21st Century, learner-centered environments that are authentic and relevant to students. The Coach Mentor understands the connection between and among all aspects of the PA Department of Education's Standards-Aligned System and its relationship to local, regional and national initiatives. The Coach Mentor is an active listener who respects confidentiality and models effective relationship-building.

Role of the Coach Mentor —*continued*	A Coach Mentor assists with the design and implementation of instructional coaches' professional development opportunities provided by the school, district, intermediate unit, and, where applicable, PDE. These opportunities include, but are not limited to, face-to-face workshops, webinars and written materials. A Coach Mentor communicates regularly with key stakeholders including IU peers and supervisor, school and district personnel, and, where applicable, PDE personnel. Coach Mentors regularly visit school sites to provide feedback to instructional coaches about the implementation and results of SAS. The Coach mentor is the primary resource for instructional coaches when there is a question or concern about implementing instructional coaching.
Non-Supervisory/ Nonevaluative	The role of the Coach Mentor is separate and apart from the supervisory and evaluative roles of the district, school, department or program administrators. The Coach Mentor advocates for, facilitates and supports the work of the instructional coach, but never performs supervisory or evaluative functions. Administrators with supervisory and evaluative roles should never solicit information from, nor should it be offered by, the Coach Mentor related to personnel matters, including informal commentary about an instructional coach's performance. The Coach Mentor does provide consultative feedback requiring professional judgment directly to the instructional coaches with whom s/he works.

Qualifications	1. A valid PA Level II teaching certificate
	
	2. Five years teaching experience with evidence of strong instructional practices
	    a. Evidence of implementing research-based instructional practices resulting in improved student achievement
	    b. Specific knowledge of, evidence of use with students, and the ability to articulate why reading, writing, speaking and listening skills and strategies are critical components of classroom instruction
	    c. Demonstrated skills in collecting, organizing and analyzing data to inform instructional decisions
	    d. Knowledge of teacher resources available in various content areas
	    e. Knowledge of and experience working with diverse learners, including English Language Learners, gifted, students with IEPs, homeless and other at-risk populations
	
	3. Experience planning and facilitating professional learning opportunities, which may include providing support to teachers through instructional coaching, mentoring, professional development, technical assistance, and/or classroom demonstrations, as well as workshops and online staff development sessions
	    a. Knowledge and application of adult learning theory

Qualifications —*continued*	4. Demonstrated competency in a leadership role
	  a. Evidence of program management and organizational skills
	  b. Demonstrated skills in problem solving, listening, collaboration and diplomacy
	  c. Excellent oral, written communications, and interpersonal skills with the ability to communicate with a variety of audiences, including teachers, administrators, school boards and parents
	  d. Demonstrated ability to facilitate, manage and direct school reform processes
	
	5. Knowledge of current state and national education initiatives targeted at improved student engagement and achievement
	  a. Knowledge and experience working with PA Standards-Aligned System, including the demonstrated ability to apply the concepts and tools associated with each element individually and to synthesize the interrelationships collectively
	  b. Experience using PDE's school improvement planning tools, including *eStrategic Plan* and *Getting Results*
	
	6. Demonstrated facility with current technology tools for instruction, communication, and office applications
	
	7. Commitment to lifelong learning, including a demonstrated passion for exploring new ideas
	
	Master's Degree, Master's Equivalency, or comparable credentials demonstrating a commitment to maintaining current knowledge and continual improvement of teaching required.

Responsibilities	1. Conducts regularly scheduled site visits to each school in which instructional coaches are located. 2. Provides one-to-one mentoring support to individual coaches. 3. Collaborates with the school leadership team to identify the school's teaching and learning needs by analyzing appropriate data and developing a plan that articulates problem-solving actions and goals—in coordination with other district, IU or PDE personnel associated with the individual school or district's planning processes. 4. Facilitates high quality professional development for coaches, administrators, teachers and others to address identified instructional needs. 5. Engages in reflective practice and supports each coach to examine and reflect on his/her practice as well.

Responsibilities —*continued*	6. Provides resources and support for the coaches as they plan and lead professional study groups.
	7. Supports coaches as they monitor student achievement data to determine the impact of instructional strategies on the learning of all students.
	8. Builds confidential relationships with the coaches to maintain a high level of trust between the coach and mentor.
	9. Participates in professional development activities that enhance knowledge of research-based instructional practices across all subject areas and to improve mentoring skills.
	10. Assists coaches and administrators with the identification of materials, tools and information that supports effective instruction.
	11. Collaborates with and supports coaches in planning and implementing Standards-Aligned Systems to improve student achievement.
	12. Develops effective procedures for communicating information about the impact of coaching on student learning to the entire school community.
	13. Maintains records of contacts and activities with school-based coaches.
	14. Provides data relative to the efficacy of the Coach Mentor role.
Professional Development for the Coach Mentor	The Coach Mentor must continually work to improve his/her practice. Therefore, the Coach Mentor should be supported in pursuing those professional development opportunities that provide the means to stay current in all aspects of the research and practices associated with the qualifications and responsibilities described herein.
Coach Mentor Relationships	Coach Mentors need to work very deliberately to establish excellent relationships with a variety of professionals. Most importantly, establishing a trusting relationship with the instructional coaches with whom they work.
Supervision of Coach Mentor	The Coach Mentor would typically report to a district central office administrator (if a district level position) or an intermediate unit Act 93 supervisor or director (if an IU position).

Source: Pennsylvania Department of Education Collaborative Coaching Board—http://www.education.pa.gov/Documents/Teachers-Administrators/Instructional%20Coaching%20in%20PA/Job%20Description%20for%20Coach%20Mentor.pdf

Bibliography

Barkley, S. (2010). *Quality teaching in a culture of coaching* (2nd ed.). Lanham, MD: Rowman & Littlefield.

Bean, R. M. (2004). Promoting effective literacy instruction: The challenge for literacy coaches. *The California Reader, 37*(3), 58–63.

Bean, R. M., and Ippolito, J. (2016). *Cultivating coaching mindsets: An action guide for literacy leaders.* West Palm Beach, FL: Learning Sciences International.

Berry, B., et al. (2011). *Teaching 2030: What we must do for our students and our public schools—now and in the future.* New York: Teachers College Press.

Charner, I., & Mean, M. (2015). *Pennsylvania Institute for Instructional Coaching (PIIC) teacher and coach survey report.* Washington, DC: FHI 360.

Cooper, D. (n.d.). *Professional development: An effective research-based model.* New York: Houghton Mifflin, Harcourt Professional Development.

Costa, A. L., & Garmston, R. J. (2002*). Cognitive coaching: A foundation for renaissance schools.* Norwood, MA: Christopher-Gordon, Inc.

Costa, A. L., & Garmston, R. J. (2016). *Cognitive coaching: Developing self-directed leaders and learners* (3rd ed.). Lanham, MD: Rowman & Littlefield.

Crane, T. G. (2012). *The heart of coaching: Using transformational coaching to create a high-performance coaching culture.* San Diego: FTA Press.

Darling-Hammond, L., Chung Wei, R., Andree, A., Richardson, N., & Orphanos, S. (2009). *Professional learning in the learning profession: A status report on teacher development in the United States and abroad.* Dallas, TX: National Staff Development Council.

Grissmer, D. W., Beekman, J. A., & Ober, D. R. (2014, February). Focusing on short-term achievement gains fails to produce long-term gains. *Education Policy Analysis Archives, 22*(5), 5. ISSN 1068–2341. Retrieved from http://epaa.asu.edu/ojs/article/view/1218

Grissom, J. A., Loeb, S., & Master, B. (2013). Effective instructional time use for school leaders: Longitudinal evidence from observations of principals. *Educational Researcher, 42*(8), 433–444. Retrieved from http://cepa.stanford.edu/content/effective-instructional-time-use-school-leaders-longitudinal-evidence-observations-principals

Gulamhussein, A. (2013). *Teaching the teachers: Effective professional development in an era of high stakes accountability.* Washington, DC: Center for Public Education. Retrieved from http://www.centerforpubliceducation.org/Main-Menu/Staffingstudents/Teaching-the-Teachers-

Effective-Professional-Development-in-an-Era-of-High-Stakes-Accountability/Teaching-the-Teachers-Full-Report.pdf

Hirsh, S. (2014, April 29). Teacher Blog Post. Does culture eat strategy for lunch? *Education Week, 23*. Retrieved from http://blogs.edweek.org/edweek/learning_forwards_pd_watch/2014/04/does_culture_eat_strategy_for_lunch.html

Institute of Leadership and Management. (2011, May). *Creating a coaching culture.* London: Institute of Leadership and Management. Retrieved from https://www.i-l-m.com/~/media/ILM%20Website/Downloads/Insight/Reports_from_ILM_website/G443_ILM_COACH_REP%20pdf.ashx

Joyce, B. R., & Showers, B. (1988). *Student achievement through staff development.* New York: Longman.

Joyce, B. R., & Showers, B. (2002). *Student achievement through staff development* (3rd ed.). Alexandria, VA: ASCD.

Killion, J., & Harrison, C. (2006). *Taking the lead: New roles for teachers and school-based coaches.* Oxford, OH: National Staff Development Council.

Killion, J., Harrison, C., Bryan, C., & Clifton, H. (2012). *Coaching matters.* Oxford, OH: Learning Forward.

Learning Forward. (2008, July). Definition of professional development. Retrieved from http://learningforward.org/who-we-are/professional-learning-definition#.VrUO81KYeW0

Loughran, J. J. (2002, January/February). Effective reflective practice: In search of meaning in learning about teaching. *Journal of Teacher Education, 53*(1), 33–43.

Mali, T. (2002). What teachers make. In T. Mali, *What learning leaves* (pp. 28–29). Newtown, CT: Hanover Press.

Medrich, E. A. (2013). PAHSCI coaching and student outcomes: "The Philadelphia story." Berkeley, CA: MPR Associates, Inc. Retrieved from http://piic.pacoaching.org/images/PIICdocuments/the%20philadelphia%20story.pdf

Medrich, E., & Charner, I. (2007). Summary of selected results from the Pennsylvania High School Coaches Initiative teachers survey. Narberth, PA: Pennsylvania High School Coaching Initiative.

Medrich, E., Fitzgerald, R., & Skomsvold, P. (2013). *Instructional coaching and student outcomes: Findings from a three-year pilot study.* Berkeley, CA.: MPR Associates.

Mulholland, J., & Turnock, C. (2013). *Learning in the workplace: A toolkit for facilitating learning and assessment in health and social care settings.* New York: Routledge.

Osterman, K. F. (1990, February). Reflective practice: A new agenda for education. *Education and Urban Society, 22*(2), 133–152. Retrieved from http://isites.harvard.edu/fs/docs/icb.topic872691.files/Osterman1990pp133-152.pdf

O'Toole, S., & Essex, B. (2012, April). The adult learner may really be a neglected species. *Australian Journal of Adult Learning, 52*(1), 183–191.

Pennsylvania Department of Education. (n.d.). Guidelines for the coach mentor position. Pennsylvania Department of Education, Collaborative Coaching Board. Retrieved from http://www.education.pa.gov/Documents/Teachers-Administrators/Instructional%20Coaching%20in%20PA/Job%20Description%20for%20Coach%20Mentor.pdf

Pennsylvania Department of Education. (n.d.). Job description for coaches in Pennsylvania coaching initiatives. Retrieved from http://www.education.pa.gov/Documents/Teachers-Administrators/Instructional%20Coaching%20in%20PA/Job%20Description%20for%20Coaches%20in%20Pennsylvania%20Coaching%20Initiatives.pdf

Pennsylvania Institute for Instructional Coaching. (2016). Retrieved from www.instituteforinstructionalcoaching.org; and www.cultureofcoaching.blogspot.com

Resnick, L. (2003). Foreword in L. West & F. C. Staub, *Content-focused coaching*. Portsmouth, NH: Heinemann.

Schön, D. A. (1983). *The reflective practitioner: How professionals think in action*. New York: Basic Books.

Schön, D. A. (1987). *Educating the reflective practitioner*. San Francisco: Jossey-Bass.

U.S. Department of Education, National Center for Education Statistics. (2016, Fall). *Fast Facts*.

Index

Note: The letter *f* following a page number denotes a figure.

About the Authors

**Ellen B. Eisenberg** is the Executive Director of the Pennsylvania Institute for Instructional Coaching (PIIC). Established in 2009, PIIC is supported by the Annenberg Foundation and the Pennsylvania Department of Education. It is a statewide resource for developing and supporting the delivery of consistent, high-quality professional development around instructional coaching and mentoring. Her work involves helping school districts plan an effective instructional coaching model built on PIIC's *before-during-after* (BDA) cycle of consultation and the four-quadrant framework of effective core coaching elements.

Ellen's experience with instructional coaching evolved through her 35-year teaching career and includes working with a whole-school reform model designed by Johns Hopkins University from 2000 to 2005, followed by her work as the Executive Director of the Pennsylvania High School Coaching Initiative (PAHSCI) from 2005 to 2009. Funded by the Annenberg Foundation, it was the nation's only multi-tiered teacher coaching initiative—providing trained teacher-leaders, called coaches, to high schools across Pennsylvania. She has authored and coauthored several articles and has presented several times locally, nationally, and internationally.

**Bruce P. Eisenberg** is the Associate Director of the Pennsylvania Institute for Instructional Coaching (PIIC). His career has spanned 47 years in public education. The first 32 years were spent teaching mathematics in a public high school where he designed and implemented curriculum for academically, musically, and artistically talented students.

Following his teaching career, Eisenberg was a consultant to the Johns Hopkins University's Talent Development High School model, where his major focus was to facilitate the restructuring of low-performing high schools around the country. From 2006 to 2009, he was a consultant with the Pennsylvania High School Coaching Initiative (PAHSCI), a partnership between the Annenberg Foundation and the Pennsylvania Department of Education. His major focus was outreach and advocacy to local, state, and federal elected officials in the legislative and executive branches of government sharing data about student achievement and job-embedded teacher professional development.

Bruce became the Associate Director of PIIC in 2009. He continues in his role of advocacy and outreach as well as in the implementation of the PIIC instructional coaching and mentoring model throughout Pennsylvania and other states.

Elliott A. Medrich is a Research Consultant to the Pennsylvania Institute for Instructional Coaching. He has been a part of PIIC's research and evaluation team for a decade. For 25 years he served as a Principal Researcher and Vice President at MPR Associates Inc., education research and policy analysts based in Berkeley, California. His 40-year career has focused on a great range of issues: designing systems and surveys for student and school-level data collection; evaluating classroom instructional practice and student outcomes; and conducting program evaluations of education initiatives at the national, state, and local levels. Medrich, who received his PhD from the University of California, Berkeley, has been an adjunct professor in the Graduate School of Public Policy, University of California, Berkeley, and has authored two books and many peer-reviewed journal articles and government publications.

Ivan Charner is the Director of the FHI 360 National Institute for Work and Learning. He is a domestic education and workforce development specialist with almost 40 years of experience in the design, development, and management of projects and programs dealing with educational policy, teacher education and professional development, college and career readiness, workforce development, and systemic reform. He works with state and local school systems, higher education institutions, corporations, government agencies, and community-based organizations to integrate and improve education, training, and career-related systems. Charner's areas of expertise include career technical education; teacher training and professional development; school-to-career system building; school reform; curriculum integration; school-business partnerships; work-based learning; and adult education and training. He designs and conducts training workshops, seminars, and conferences, is a regular presenter at the American Association of Colleges of Teacher Education, and has written extensively on teacher preparation and effectiveness, youth transition from school to career, school reform, college and career readiness issues, instructional coaching, career and technical education, and school-business partnerships.